# Poetry in Motion

# Staffordshire
Edited by Chris Hallam

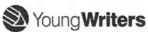 Young**Writers**

First published in Great Britain in 2004 by:
Young Writers
Remus House
Coltsfoot Drive
Peterborough
PE2 9JX
Telephone: 01733 890066
Website: www.youngwriters.co.uk

SB ISBN 1 84460 388 1

# Foreword

This year, the Young Writers' 'Poetry In Motion' competition proudly presents a showcase of the best poetic talent selected from over 40,000 up-and-coming writers nationwide.

Young Writers was established in 1991 to promote the reading and writing of poetry within schools and to the youth of today. Our books nurture and inspire confidence in the ability of young writers and provide a snapshot of poems written in schools and at home by budding poets of the future.

The thought effort, imagination and hard work put into each poem impressed us all and the task of selecting poems was a difficult but nevertheless enjoyable experience.

We hope you are as pleased as we are with the final selection and that you and your family continue to be entertained with *Poetry In Motion Staffordshire* for many years to come.

# Contents

| | |
|---|---|
| Tim Robinson  (12) | 40 |
| Claire Toman  (12) | 41 |
| Gillian Panter  (13) | 42 |
| Daniella Smith  (12) | 42 |
| Christopher Turner  (12) | 43 |
| Peter Reisner  (12) | 43 |
| Laura Nelson  (12) | 44 |
| Grace Slights  (11) | 45 |
| Hannah Slater  (13) | 46 |
| Katie Woods  (11) | 46 |
| Lucy Moody  (12) | 47 |
| Stuart Gale  (12) | 47 |
| Danielle Butler  (13) | 48 |
| Sophie Hall  (13) | 49 |
| Tanya O'Brien  (11) | 50 |
| Lauren Smith  (12) | 51 |
| Sally Burton  (13) | 52 |
| Natasha Waller  (11) | 53 |
| Lydia Hargrove  (14) | 54 |
| Hannah Dixon  (13) | 55 |
| Anna Meynell  (12) | 56 |
| Doris Ward  (12) | 57 |
| Melissa Pomlett  (11) | 58 |
| Torryn Kersey  (11) | 59 |
| George Clarke  (11) | 60 |

## Maple Hayes Dyslexia School

| | |
|---|---|
| Ryan Kavanagh  (12) | 60 |
| Bruce Dale  (12) | 61 |
| Keyston Brown  (12) | 61 |
| Daniel Garner  (12) | 62 |
| Charles Carden  (12) | 62 |

## Painsley Catholic High School

| | |
|---|---|
| Hayley Turner  (13) | 63 |
| Matthew Rowley  (14) | 63 |
| Paul Dudley  (14) | 64 |
| Danielle Hill  (14) | 64 |
| Katie Finney  (14) | 65 |
| Kirsty Dunn  (14) | 65 |
| Ross Daniels  (14) | 66 |

| | |
|---|---|
| Laura Mycock (14) | 66 |
| Charlotte Ashby (13) | 67 |
| Elizabeth Lasota (14) | 67 |
| Steven Baddeley (14) | 68 |
| Nicholas Harvey (14) | 68 |
| David Daniels (13) | 69 |
| Luke Daly (14) | 69 |
| Kamurai Wabatagore (13) | 70 |
| Matthew Capper (14) | 71 |
| Matthew Prince (14) | 71 |
| Natasha Hallam (14) | 72 |
| Rebecca Heron (14) | 73 |
| Kayleigh Allen (14) | 74 |
| Lauren Tilstone (14) | 75 |
| Natalie Wolff (14) | 76 |
| Ben Stott (14) | 76 |
| Robbi Hill (13) | 77 |
| Jamie Capper (11) | 77 |
| Adam Atkinson (13) | 78 |
| Jorge Lindley (13) | 79 |
| Charlotte Gumny (13) | 80 |
| Amy Whitehurst (11) | 80 |
| Martin Bland (14) | 81 |
| Natasha Ekin (14) | 81 |
| Lucy Wrightson (14) | 82 |
| Patrick Floyd (14) | 82 |
| Chris Moult (13) | 83 |
| Natalie Hudson (14) | 83 |
| Laura Simpson (14) | 84 |
| Emma Lawton (13) | 84 |
| Sarah Rushton (14) | 85 |
| Hayley Fearn (13) | 85 |
| Alexander Humphreys (14) | 86 |
| Luke Bath (13) | 86 |
| Victoria Lamburn (13) | 87 |
| Kate Buttress (12) | 87 |
| Philip Long (14) | 88 |
| Andrew Williamson (13) | 88 |
| Oonagh Scannell (14) | 89 |
| Joseph Earley (14) | 89 |
| Mark Deighton (14) | 90 |
| Charlotte Priddey (13) | 91 |

| | |
|---|---|
| Hannah Mycock  (14) | 92 |
| Nicolas Shaw  (12) | 92 |
| Harriet Collier  (12) | 93 |
| Thomas Arme  (13) | 93 |
| Matthew Forrester  (11) | 94 |
| Marie Insley  (13) | 95 |
| Tom Bland  (11) | 96 |
| Lucy Offen  (13) | 96 |
| Alexandra Foulkes  (11) | 97 |
| Jake Jeffs  (11) | 97 |
| Katie Shield  (13) | 98 |
| Matthew Hurst  (14) | 98 |
| Sarah Lockett  (14) | 99 |
| Katy Warrilow  (14) | 99 |
| Emily Dixon  (11) | 100 |
| Kerry McMullen  (14) | 100 |
| Stacey Greener  (14) | 101 |
| Jessica Hackett  (13) | 102 |
| Jade Cartwright  (13) | 103 |
| Alex Watson-Lazowski  (13) | 104 |
| Nicola Ball  (13) | 104 |
| Jade Goodwin  (14) | 105 |
| Hayley Finney  (12) | 105 |
| Philip Milward  (15) | 106 |
| Zoe Slater  (13) | 107 |
| Lorna Poole  (15) | 108 |
| James Phillips  (14) | 108 |
| Tabatha Snow  (13) | 109 |
| Victoria Deaville  (13) | 109 |
| Amy Dowling  (13) | 110 |
| Rosemarie Brown  (11) | 110 |
| Alison Eardley  (13) | 111 |
| Zoe Hewitt  (14) | 111 |
| Sam Barcham  (13) | 112 |
| Paul Whalley  (13) | 112 |
| Matthew Sargeant  (11) | 113 |
| Natalie McCall  (13) | 113 |
| Katie Cooper  (13) | 114 |
| Aaron Coleman  (13) | 114 |
| Kirsty Buckley  (13) | 115 |
| Alexander Bamford  (11) | 115 |
| Eloise Whitehall  (11) | 116 |

## Queen Elizabeth's Mercian School

| | |
|---|---|
| Abbie-May Robinson  (11) | 190 |
| Jamie Glynn  (12) | 190 |
| Connor Deacon  (11) | 191 |
| Hayley Murkett  (16) | 191 |
| Emma Fitzpatrick  (15) | 192 |
| Stephen Corden  (11) | 192 |
| Tom Mortimer  (11) | 193 |
| Sam Jones  (12) | 193 |
| Victoria Thorpe  (11) | 194 |
| Thomas McLaughlin  (11) | 194 |
| Amie Azarzar  (11) | 195 |
| Jack Asbury  (11) | 195 |
| Amy Simmons  (11) | 196 |
| Damien Fitzpatrick  (11) | 197 |
| Ben Watson  (11) | 197 |
| Nathan Burns  (11) | 198 |
| Matthew Hutchinson  (11) | 198 |
| Jessica Lobo  (11) | 199 |
| Stephen Ashe  (11) | 199 |
| Dominic Williscroft  (11) | 199 |

## Quince Tree Special School

| | |
|---|---|
| Lee Grieves  (17) | 200 |
| Brett Jennings  (15) | 200 |
| Donna Allen  (15) | 201 |
| Craig Berrow  (17) | 201 |
| Katie Aucote  (17) | 202 |
| Brian Hanslow  (15) | 202 |
| Alex Thomas  (17) | 202 |
| Samantha McIntyre  (15) | 203 |
| Kay Ward  (16) | 203 |
| Joseph Ball  (15) | 204 |
| Mark Brotherton  (15) | 204 |

## St Francis of Assisi Roman Catholic School

| | |
|---|---|
| Robert Cregeen  (16) | 205 |
| Scott Davies  (11) | 206 |
| David Shaw  (15) | 206 |
| Claire Plunkett  (12) | 207 |
| Jade Kent-Williams  (11) | 207 |

## The Rawlett High School

# The Poems

# Teenage Angst

When adults complain of feeling pressure,
It's usually down to bills or the weather,
But when teenage girls like me get mad,
The cause is usually Mum or Dad.
Without our parents, life would be,
A time of peace and tranquillity.
No petty rules, no early to bed,
No one to tell me to use my head.
No one to say, 'Is your homework done?'
No one to say, 'Tie your hair in a bun.'
No one to tell me to 'Eat more fruit.'
No one to tell me my face looks cute.
Without our parents, life would be,
A time of peace and tranquillity.
For a girl like me it would be heaven,
To go to bed at half-past eleven.
To raid the fridge at any time,
To drink my parents' expensive wine,
To wear my skirt above the knee,
To scoff on chocolate for my tea.
Without our parents, life would be,
A time of peace and tranquillity.
Exams would be a thing of the past,
I'd play my music on full blast,
But when life is good and I am having fun,
Round the corner lurks Dad and Mum.
Though girls may have their faults of course,
Our problems stem from one main source,
Without our parents, life would be,
A time of peace and tranquillity.

**Tiffany Hubbard  (15)**
**Alleynes High School**

# In A Small Glass Box

In a small glass box
There's nowhere to hide
I can't get out
Chains surrounding my frail body
Cutting into my wrists
Bleeding dark blood
Fresh, dark blood
I scream but no one hears me
The small glass box
Getting smaller
Smaller
I can't get out!
The box fills up with blood
My blood
I'm drowning
Drowning in my oozing liquid
In the small glass box
Where nobody can get in or out
Lies a corpse
The corpse of myself
Bleeding still
But silently now
No one knew me
No one heard me
But it doesn't matter now
Now that I'm dead . . .

**Amy Holihead  (15)**
**Alleynes High School**

# A New Moon

A new moon shone tonight,
I watched it as it came so bright.
I stood on the beach in Italy,
The sea as white as it could be.
I walked so sad across the sands,
Towards the sound of the brass bands.
Far from the rushing sound I fled,
To find some sand inside my bed.
I felt the moon shine in my eyes,
I said goodbye to a moon that cries.
I held the moon and stopped its tears
And promised it my future years.

The same moon now shines at home,
I stand and watch it quite alone.
I feel the sand and see the sky
And only wish that I could fly.
Back to those rushing waves before,
That beat on my Italian shore.

**Jane Hand (18)**
**Alleynes High School**


# The Movement Of The Wind

The direction in which the wind blows,
Manipulates and shapes the way the river flows.

The effect and speed of the winter breeze
Chills everything and makes it freeze.

The wind can blow fierce and strong or a gust
And can blow lots of dust.

The wind stops after it blows the leaves in a pile,
Because it rests for a while.

**Glenn Clark (11)**
**Brewood CE Middle School**

# Sir Ed

I saw a young boy walking down the street,
I asked him his name and this is what he said,
'My name is Edward
And I come from Brewood,
I live on Deansfield Road
And I have a dog who reminds me of you.
I'm Sir Ed, Sir Ed is my name,
I live in 13 Hall,
I own a dog who is my delight.
Yes, Sir Ed, Sir Ed,
My dad is a king,
My mother is a queen
And my sister is a pain in the wall.'
I said goodbye and I knew I would
Never see him again.

**Martin Hayes (11)**
**Brewood CE Middle School**


# The Baby Dolphin

The dolphin swims in the wavy sea,
Flicking its tail up at me.
Dolphin dives under the water,
I stare into the deep sea.

Then the dolphin shoots out of the sea,
Guess what? He wet me!
Then starts getting gentler,
I turn around and there's my mum,
She says, 'It's time for tea.'

I get up and start to walk away,
I hear a noise and turn to see,
There's the dolphin doing somersaults for me.

**Nikola Clarke (11)**
**Brewood CE Middle School**

# Wintertime

W inter is a time for mistletoe and wine
    and children playing in the snow having fun
    then the redbreast robin watching them play in the snow
    and he flies, flies, flies away

I n the wintertime there is no school
    so all the children are very happy
    and they run and play in the snow
    and make snowballs and snow angels

N ovember is in the wintertime
    when it's Bonfire Night everyone has to remember
    remember the fifth of November

T uck up nice and snug with your favourite teddy bear
    and a mug of hot chocolate
    and sit around the fire and switch on the television
    and watch your favourite programme

E at a turkey round the table with family and friends
    and pour the gravy all over the turkey and munch, munch, munch

R un, run as fast as you can
    because it is starting to snow
    and it is freezing cold.

**Joshua Hodgkins  (11)**
**Brewood CE Middle School**


# Winter

W ind blows the leaves off the trees
 I n the winter snow might come down
N ever wear shorts or a T-shirt
T he winter makes me shiver
E vergreen trees grow in the winter
R eptiles hibernate.

**Emilio Dicesare  (11)**
**Brewood CE Middle School**

# The Team

The leaves were falling,
The children were running
And it was pouring down with rain.

Whistles were whistling,
The leaves were rustling,
The children were freezing away.

The footballs were out
And the kit was cold,
The ground was muddy too.

The rain had cleared,
The sun had come out,
The team was picked by the coach.

**Christopher Wiles (11)**
**Brewood CE Middle School**


# My Dog

My dog runs around,
She wees up a tree,
She swims in the rivers,
She swims in the sea.

She fetches a stick,
She fetches a ball,
She walks around,
She stumbles and stalls.

She'll lie on the grass,
She'll lie on the sand,
She'll lie there for ages,
With her head on my hand.

**Alex Swingwood (11)**
**Brewood CE Middle School**

# Sir Tink

When I was young, I was walking down the street,
I met with a young boy,
I asked him to tell me his name.
'My name is Sir Tink and I live at Broom Hall,
I have two guinea pigs which are my delight.
Yes!
Sir Tink, Sir Tink, Sir Tink is my name
And I live at Broom Hall,
I have two guinea pigs which are my delight.'

'Who are your family?' I asked him with care.
'My dad's a king,
My mum's a queen,
My brothers are a pain in the backside.'

So then I left him in the rocky street,
I know I shall never see him again,
'Sir Tink, Sir Tink, Sir Tink is my name
And I live at Broom Hall.'

**Edward Birtles  (11)**
**Brewood CE Middle School**

# Friends

A friend is very special
And hopefully for life,
They're there to share the good times
And see you through the strife.

It starts to form from school life
And sees it through to teens
And when you reach adulthood
You realise what friendship means.

**Thomas Scragg  (11)**
**Brewood CE Middle School**

# Apple Pie

I was walking down a path last night,
Going home from school,
When a lion came out of nowhere,
Made me jump like a fool.

It chased me up and down the path,
Through a garden hedge,
I screamed just like my little sis,
Then spotted a window ledge.

I ran and ran as fast as I could,
Till my legs gave way and fell,
Then the lion pounced on me,
It felt as if I'd fallen down a well.

The lion started licking me,
I really wondered why,
My eyes then opened fully wide,
Phew! It was just my dog, Apple Pie.

**Lucy Cumming  (12)**
**Brewood CE Middle School**

# Snake

I have a pet snake,
Who likes to eat cake,
He slithers around my town
And sometimes hides in my mum's nightgown.

He knows some good jokes,
But insults my folks,
He's a very rude snake
And can swim in a lake.

He went in my dad's shed
And nearly lost his head,
Because he knocked over an axe,
When slithering over some tacks.

**Oliver Sorsby  (11)**
**Brewood CE Middle School**

# Winter's Come

The day has arrived
the winter has come
the ponds are frozen
and there's no harm done

Everything has stopped moving
the liveliness has died
the breakfast is cooked
and the eggs are fried

The snow is now falling
the colour begins to fade
the snow has covered everything
and the snowmen are made

Christmas is now coming
the lights are up
all the little boys and girls
just want a little pup

So here it is, Christmas Day
the turkey's being cooked
the children have opened all the presents
and the wrapping overlooked.

**Stephen Hawkins  (11)**
**Brewood CE Middle School**

# Which Witch?

I wonder which witch is in my attic?
Making that noise is becoming a habit!
Is it the one with the pointy black hat
Or is it the one with the tabby cat?
Shall I go up there? Shall I be brave?
Shall I go up there and stop all that rave?
Now I've made up my own choice,
I'm going to go up there to raise my voice!

**Rebecca Lloyd  (11)**
**Brewood CE Middle School**

# The Woods

All is still in the woods,
There stood a man with his dog,
Something moves in the shadows,
What could it be? What could it be?

The man starts moving,
The dog starts growling,
The thing starts backing away,
What could it be? What could it be?

The man starts running,
The dog starts barking,
The thing starts running,
What could it be? What could it be?

The man starts jogging,
The dog starts leaping,
The thing picks up speed,
What could it be? What could it be?

The man starts racing,
The dog starts fiercely jumping,
The thing starts darting,
What could it be? What could it be?

**Jenny Morgan  (11)**
**Brewood CE Middle School**


# As The Time Goes By

The river runs slowly
The jaguar runs fast
The hours pass by
And the days don't last
The seasons are ever changing
And seem to merge into one
As the time goes by . . .

**Gina Padilla  (12)**
**Brewood CE Middle School**

# The Seasons

*Spring*
Daffodils dancing daintily
Lambs leaping lazily
Buds bursting beautifully

*Summer*
Heat, haze, holidays
Beaches, burns and burgers
Sun, sand, sea

*Autumn*
Golden, glorious, gorgeous
Crunchy, crispy, crackly
Bonfires burning brightly

*Winter*
Crispy, clean
First footsteps follow
Dirty, despair, disappointment, death.

**Daniel Vaughan  (11)**
**Brewood CE Middle School**

# Rain

Outside I can see the rain,
It's dripping and dropping a lot.
It's making pools of water now,
Oh how I wish it would stop.

Outside is the rain,
It's getting harder you see.
It's running down the drainpipe now,
It won't be long, soon in fact we will be under a sea.

Outside there's no rain,
It's stopped now you see.
So I can play outside again
And I'll be in for tea.

**Charlotte Faulkner  (11)**
**Brewood CE Middle School**

# I'll Be Late For School!

I leapt out of bed this morning,
As my bed shouted,'*Come on, come back to bed and relax,*'
'I can't,' I said, 'I'll be late for school!'

I ran past the fridge
As it groaned *'Open me and get some breakfast,*'
'I can't, I yelled, 'I'll be late for school!'

I walked by some flowers,
As they moaned *'Water me,'*
I continued walking as I cried,
'I can't, I'm going to be late for school!'

I finally got to the school gate,
As it said *'Open me,'*
'I will or I'll be late for school!'
I sighed.

**Becky Markham  (12)**
**Brewood CE Middle School**

# The Winter Season!

Winter is wonderful especially when snowy,
But better wrap up warmly or it will be too blowy.
Make sure you have a snowball fight,
Make it last till it becomes the dead of night.

See the moon from way high above,
If you can, it will be a marvellous sight.
Look! Undone your lace,
Ha! There's a snowball in your face!

You have enjoyed a wonderful day,
Imagine the different weather if you were in May!
Go back home and huddle round the fire,
Hope you enjoyed my winter poem!

**James Pugh  (11)**
**Brewood CE Middle School**

# Fog!

Black!
White!
A mystic feather

Icy!
Blurred!
He blocks your sight

Fighter!
Aggressive!
The sun fights back

Old!
Ancient!
An old enemy of the sun

Clear!
Claustrophobic!
Chokes everything in sight

Finally!
Ending!
The fog rolls away.

**Charlotte Pugh (11)**
**Brewood CE Middle School**


# Bubbles

Bubbles, bubbles, bubbles,
Floating up, left and right,
Until they're all out of sight.

Bubbles, bubbles, bubbles,
Slowly falling to the ground,
Softly moving without a sound.

Bubbles, bubbles, bubbles,
Shiny and round,
Until they hit the stone-cold ground.

**Shauni Danby (11)**
**Brewood CE Middle School**

# The Sea

The rushing waves of the sea,
Crashing, splashing everywhere,
Oh now I wish I was there.
The tide is in, there's no escape,
Oh now the shell beneath my feet,
Oh how I wish I had something to eat.
It's Sunday night, the shops are closed,
Silence, I can only hear the sound of the sea
And people having their tea.
The moon is shining above the sea,
Sparkling, glittering, shining like mad,
Then I open my eyes to see,
I'm in bed and not by the sea.
Then my mum brings me in a cup of tea,
But I can still hear the sound of the sea,
The graceful waves going back and forward.
I can feel the sand beneath my feet
And the cold breeze in my hair,
Oh how I wish I was there.

**Alex Shore (11)**
**Brewood CE Middle School**


# Steam

Steam
A very powerful thing
It turns the wheels on the massive locomotives
It turns the steamroller's roller
But if the pressure gets too high
*Boom*
Up you'll go

So have the boilers fitted with safety valves
If you want to live
Steam is a very powerful thing.

**Ben Hatton (11)**
**Brewood CE Middle School**

# Footie Fantastic

Footballs, footballs everywhere
Right up here and right down there
Where you turn there is one there
Footballs, footballs everywhere

Ryan Giggs, Ryan Giggs, he is famous
Wherever he is Ryan Giggs scores a goal
All you hear is great big cheers

Players, players everywhere
Over here and over there

Managers, managers everywhere
Right up here and right down there
Shouting, 'Pass, pass, cross, cross
Go and show them who's boss.'

**Grant Hassall (11)**
**Brewood CE Middle School**


# Seasons Changing

Spring flowers begin to open
Sun shining in the summer
Green leaves turn to orange
Autumn leaves begin to fall
Snow drifting in the winter
Seasons change from day to night

Farmers watching lambs be born
Adults relaxing in the sun
Children rolling in the leaves
People playing in the snow
Seasons change from season to season.

**Sarah Bond (11)**
**Brewood CE Middle School**

# Bullying!

The day my life changed
I was walking through the playground
I couldn't find my friends
A boy came over to me

He was tall and thin
He had blond hair
And brown beady eyes
I was afraid, he started to talk
I opened my packet of crisps

'Give me those,' he said loudly
I gave him the crisps
He pushed me around, I hit my head
Suddenly my friends came over

He might be a friend to someone
But I never shall mention his name.

**Hannah Palmer (11)**
**Brewood CE Middle School**


# My Little Sister

My little sister is a little girl,
She has straight hair and one tiny curl,
She's dainty and sweet,
The type of person you'd like to meet.

My little sister can cause a lot of trouble
And can be great to give a cuddle,
She has eyes of emeralds and pearls,
But don't let her fool you - she sends our family up in whirls.

Her neck is short and her teeth are big,
Her hair is silky and doesn't need a wig,
Her eyes are a shade of the sky,
Sometimes she can tell a lie or maybe you would call it a porky pie!

**Grace Hupperdine (11)**
**Brewood CE Middle School**

# In The Deep Blue Sea

Under, over, around the side,
I wonder where I will hide?
I see straight ahead,
Nice and cosy, a bed.

I swim above, then below,
I make a choice as I know,
I decide to go under the bed,
I find all sorts lurking under there.

The smell tickling up my nose,
Suddenly a flash of red rose,
As you may have guessed what I am,
I am a dolphin playing in the deep blue sea.

I have fun with Freddy my friend,
We all hope our friendship will never end.

I love to seek and hide,
I then open my mouth wide
And sneeze, the game is over,
I have been found.

**Amy Wilkins  (11)**
**Brewood CE Middle School**


# The Splashing Dolphins

Dolphins are friendly, they live in the sea,
They play with their friends but where could they be?
I wish I could have a dolphin to play with me
And one of the dolphins is called Lee.

The dolphins were jumping out of the sea with glee,
But Lee got stuck in a net and Josh helped him free.
Chloé was playing with her ball when she saw a flea
And Alice was jumping through a hoop when she fell in the cold sea.

**Samantha Hicks  (11)**
**Brewood CE Middle School**

# My Love For Music!

My love for music is like never before,
Singing in my bedroom or on the dance floor,
Knocking everyone out so they want to hear more,
Years to come fans will be knocking at my door.

I want a good singing career,
Fans coming from both far and near,
Singing on stage year after year,
People coming to me just to hear.

I need to sing, I just can't bear it,
Such a craving, I can't get over it,
People coming just to see and hear it,
Fans asking for autographs, I'm so proud of it.

Hearing fans sing along to my tune,
I won't give up even when I look like a prune,
When I sing I feel like I'm jumping over the moon,
When I go on tour I say to my fans, 'I'll be back soon.'

**Alisha Gibson  (11)**
**Brewood CE Middle School**


# Cats For You

Cats can be black, white or any colour you like
Not pink or green, that's just mean
Not orange or blue
They won't have a clue
They like meat or biscuits
You could get a tabby
A long-haired or short-haired
Just give them attention
What kind would you like?
The choice is up to you.

**Ellie Mason  (11)**
**Brewood CE Middle School**

# A Terrible Night

It was a stormy night
The lightning gave her a fright.
She heard cars screeching
And children screaming,
It was a terrible, terrible night.

Sirens were sounding,
Feet were pounding,
She was all alone,
Her mom was not home,
It was a terrible, terrible night.

Trees were rustling,
People were bustling,
The lights in the street were out,
She heard a great big shout,
It was a terrible, terrible night.

**Chloe Yerlett (11)**
**Brewood CE Middle School**

# Football

Footballs racing across the field,
Grass ending everywhere,
Football players hurting their knees,
Paramedics racing on the pitch,
People's legs in cast,
People's fingernails half off,
People tripping over the ball,
Footballers' clothes hanging from them, nearly falling off,
People throwing tomatoes and cabbages,
People falling off their chairs when their team scores,
What sort of *game* do you call that?

**Naomi Pitt (11)**
**Brewood CE Middle School**

# Mummy And Daddy

They were there for a while,
All of them wearing a smile.
They both left the room,
Heading straight to doom.
They left her alone,
Their smiles no longer shone,
She went to live with her grandparents,
As she no longer had her parents.
At four years old,
Her life seemed incredibly cold.
Her brother was there,
But her life didn't seem fair,
As her parents weren't there,
She was right.
As she grew old,
She became more bold
And learnt to survive on her own (she thought),
Her heart had grown,
She was in fact no longer alone,
She had her brother
And grandparents,
But she never had the chance to know or say,
'Mummy and Daddy.'

**Kirsten Hayes  (11)**
**Brewood CE Middle School**


# Dragons

Dragons, dragons, fiery dragons,
With their sharp clawed teeth,
Running round with their fierce feet,
Dragons have those beastly eyes
Which glare from a distance,
To catch human lives.

**Natalie Springthorpe  (11)**
**Brewood CE Middle School**

# Weather

Some people are like fire,
Tearing through other lives,
Destroying them
And then burning out.

Other people are like water,
They put out the fire,
Even when it comes back
Again and again.

A few people are like hurricanes,
They blow through life,
Making a mess of things,
That can't be put right.

There are people who are like hail,
Hard but made up of lots of things,
Those people hurt,
Then they realise and stop.

A lot of people are like a gentle wind,
They breeze through life,
Only picking up some rubbish,
But they soon drop it again.

Many people are like sunshine,
They bring brightness into the world,
Brightening up people's lives
And they always block out the rainy days.

What are you like
Fire, water, a hurricane, hail
A slight wind or do you bring sunshine
To people's rainy days?

**Ellis Chatter  (11)**
**Brewood CE Middle School**

# Butterflies

Butterflies fly
On summer days
Butterflies fly
In different ways

Landing on a flower
Flying in the trees
Crawling in the grass
Or fluttering in the breeze

Butterflies are
So colourful
Butterflies are
So graceful

Their wings have patterns
They're small in size
Their legs are thin
They're butterflies!

**Sarah Johnson  (12)**
**Brewood CE Middle School**


# The Sea And The Sand

The sea and the sand are the best of friends,
The sea to the human eye never ends.

The sand is golden and bright,
The sea glistens in the night.

The sea is soft and sometimes rough,
The sand is where young children can't get enough.

The sand is grainy with lots of shells,
The sea is smooth with salty smells.

Where the sea and the sand join is a peaceful land
And they're always hand in hand.

**Elodie Joseph  (11)**
**Brewood CE Middle School**

# Leaves In The Wind

There's a storm outside, it's getting worse,
It's raining as fast as lightning,
My little tree is blowing and has lost all its leaves
Apart from one.
It looks like it's waving to me,
A big gust of wind struck the garden,
The leaf started to fly,
*Loop-the-loop*, backwards and forwards,
Up and down.
Then through the clouds, a single sunray
Appeared then another and another.
The wind dropped and so did my leaf
As though it was dead,
It lay in a puddle,
Then a rainbow cleared the clouds away.

**Charlotte Fortescue  (11)**
**Brewood CE Middle School**


# Cats

I sit on a garden wall,
I'm sleek, I'm thin, I'm tall,
I'm also very smart,
About the street I dart
And when I spot my prey,
I stalk and pounce away.
But there is one I fear
And he lives so very near,
His hair is shaggy and rough,
Humans favour him to us,
He is lazy and sleeps all day,
But chases us away,
All hours, all night, all day,
We loathe him in every way.

**Jessica Butler  (11)**
**Brewood CE Middle School**

# Monsters Before 12.00

Rain thundering down on the black seabed
Fish darting up and down
Sharks lying all around!

Argh! I scream, bolting up like lighting
'What's that, Mum? What's that?'
'Hush young James, only the thunder.'
'But, but it's making me wonder!'
'So don't you fret, go back to bed!'

'OK, Mum, I'll go back to bed
With my sleepy head.'
'Oh and darling, did I mention the monster in the sea
That comes out and eats young boys
If they don't go to bed before 12.00 . . .'
*Argh!*

**Emma Shaw  (11)**
**Brewood CE Middle School**


# Misty Hours

As we walk past the clock mounted on our wall,
We think, how long will it be before the badger puts away its paws?
How long will it be until the mist finally goes
And we wonder when the cockerel will crow?
But the darkness is still using its powers,
So we will have to wait some more long, misty hours.
When we wake, the cockerel shall have crowed
And the badger will have put away its paws,
So now there is no need to wonder,
For the misty hours shall have gone down under!

**Virginia Dabbs  (11)**
**Brewood CE Middle School**

# Mice

Their tails are very long,
Their faces are small,
They haven't any chins at all,
Their ears are pink
And their teeth are white
And they run about the house
At night.

When I go to bed at night,
They eat the crumbs that are in sight,
When they hear a noise,
They run for their life,
Under the stairs, out of sight,
To look for something else to bite
And to hide again until the time is right,
Who are we?

**Jamie Whitfield (11)**
**Brewood CE Middle School**


# Football

The match starts,
Back to defence,
They pass it to midfield,
Who move swiftly.

A pass to the right,
It's found the winger,
The defender dives in,
He's missed!

The winger's gone,
The tension mounts!
Smash! Into the box,
Wham! A volley,
*Goal!*

**Ben Jarocki (11)**
**Brewood CE Middle School**

# Witches' Broth

Squish of toad scraped from road
Whiff of dog's bad breath
Put this together and mix it well
Come and I'll tell you the rest
Spray of cat and wing of bat
Mix this in as well
A few cowpats and a tail of a rat
The potion will now start to smell
A couple of nits and a snout of a pig
Drop in a squeaky mouse too
Mugs full of hamsters, leave some for samplers
These just add in some chew
Slime of snail and bite of nails
Keep the dirt inside
Drop by drop add some spots
Again keep the pus inside

Present it nice with some eyes on the side
You now have completed your stew!

Hold it steady, your victims are now ready
Just hope they don't start to spew
Roll up your sleeves as they start to heave
And let them finish their food
Give them their bag and send them packing
And let their pants be pooed!

**Charlie Hemmings  (11)**
**Brewood CE Middle School**


# A Winter Breeze

When the flower moves with the breeze,
You might get a little sneeze,
It might sound like a tissue again,
Because you might be asleep in the rain,
So don't get more cold
Else you might sneeze again.

**Mitchell Skitt  (11)**
**Brewood CE Middle School**

# Dolphins

Dolphins dive,
Dolphins jump,
Dolphins leap,
Dolphins splash.

Dolphins are fun,
Dolphins are playful,
Dolphins like people,
People there like them.

Dolphins are great,
Dolphins are brilliant,
When they do their tricks,
Dolphins are fantastic.

*Dolphins are the best!*

**Danielle Reynolds  (11)**
**Brewood CE Middle School**

# About Me

My life is miserable
And I feel like I am going from past to future
I'm staring out the window
With not a care in the world

My boyfriend's dumped me
Now I'm all on my own
But the world goes so fast
I can't tell what time it is

My friends think they're hippies
Going out every night
While I am stuck in the house
Listening to the clock going
Tick-tock, tick-tock all night long.

**Jodie Davies  (11)**
**Brewood CE Middle School**

# Roses Are Red

Roses are red
Violets are blue
Where do I live
And what do I do?
I go home
And talk down the phone
To my friend, Bob

Roses are red
Violets are blue
Alex and Bob have had a fight
But who has won?

Roses are red
Violets are blue
Alex wins with a
Magnificent punch.

**Josh Green  (12)**
**Brewood CE Middle School**


# Storm

Water crashing on the rocks, mist forming in the sea,
Animals taking cover from the storm
And now people hiding away,
Waves forming to a mighty gust
And me in the comfort of my warm home,
Eating the finest food and animals barely finding food to survive,
Me in the warm, fire as it burns with heat and lights up the room,
Poor people looking for cover as the lightning comes down
With the rain, me under my blanket, nice and warm,
Animals can't take the lightning flash
As they are so scared and me, the most safe one of all.

**Jamie McLintock  (11)**
**Brewood CE Middle School**

# A Flower

A flower is silent,
A flower is pretty,
A flower can be happy
Or maybe sad.

A flower might sting,
A flower might heal,
A flower should be a
Way of expression.

A flower may be green,
Yellow, pink, orange, red or blue.

A flower is graceful,
A flower is large or small,
A flower is part of one
Great big world.

**Jade Hough  (11)**
**Brewood CE Middle School**


# Slow Motion Clock

*Tick-tock* the world goes by
*Tick-tock* so do I
*Ding-dong* the world has run
*Ding-dong* so I sung

*Tick-tock* school slow
*Tick-tock* I am on the go
*Ding-dong* my house is cool
*Ding-dong* it is tall

*Tick-tock* my friend and I
*Tick-tock* now we say bye
*Ding-dong* my friend has gone
*Ding-dong* the sun has shone.

**Jodie Collins  (11)**
**Brewood CE Middle School**

# Bob, Bob

Bob, bob went the fish,
Swimming in his bowl,
Going for his goal,
To have a friend.

Bob, bob, went the fish,
Racing round the bowl,
Going for his goal,
To be a racing car driver.

Bob, bob went the fish,
Staying in his bowl,
Going for his goal,
Not to move a muscle,
Because the cat was there.

**Alex Moore  (11)**
**Brewood CE Middle School**


# Waves

Waves crashing up rocks like they're on a slide,
While people quiver on the side,
Up and down and back again,
Watch all day with no pain,
Oh the clear sea,
What a beautiful sight to see,
I can't come every day,
I have to pay,
I love this place,
It's ace.

**Will Talbot  (11)**
**Brewood CE Middle School**

# Flying Dream

Flying in the sky,
With birds flashing by,
Now the sun is coming out,
We can play about.

The sun is too bright,
At a miracle height,
Then the moon comes out
And we can't play about.

Wolves were howling,
People were shouting,
'Go to bed,' she said,
I fell asleep like I was dead.

We woke up this morning
And we were falling,
We shouted, 'Help! Help! Help!'
And the chocolate started to melt.

We were falling in the sea
And I nearly landed on my knee,
Then came a magic carpet
And flew us to the market.

My friends saw Mum,
She was looking quite glum,
She said, 'Wake up, Son,
Your breakfast is done.'

I opened my eyes,
Oh what a surprise,
I had been dreaming,
So why was I screaming?

**Gareth Irvine (11)**
**Brewood CE Middle School**

# When I Went To Wales

When I went to Wales I wanted to see the sea,
I wanted to go there just Aunty, Uncle and me,
When I went to Wales I wanted to walk the land,
But because of foot-and-mouth disease
We had to stick to sea and sand.

When I went to Wales, I wanted to explore the long brown trees,
The tall grass tickling your legs as you pass.

Around the mountains I wanted to walk,
Oh no, no,
Says the law, not at the moment while there's a
Sort of thing that spreads around doing a horrible thing.

But now it's ended and all gone away,
You can go there now at night or by day,
There's lots of new trees with gold and brown leaves,
Seen as it's autumn again.

You can see birds gliding
And go horse riding,
Or maybe just breathe the fresh air.

No sign of rain,
So take the train
Around the countryside, under the tunnel,
Goes the old steam train fit with its funnel.

**Georgia Gibbon (11)**
**Brewood CE Middle School**

# Pop

Sometimes I may feel sad,
But I'll soon be flicking through my sketchpad,
It cheers me up with those cats and dogs
And teddy bears and wooden clogs,
But I always look at the sketch most dear,
My great grandad Pop, who I lost last year.

**Sarah Edgell (11)**
**Brewood CE Middle School**

# The Thunderstorm

Waves crashing, wind howling,
Waves smashing up a cliff.
The clouds crashing making it thunder,
*Bang!* went the thunder,
Lightning crashing trees down.

Far out to sea was a wreck,
The thunder hit it and set it on fire,
The wind getting stronger and louder.

Then suddenly the loudest *bang* came,
Then the wind started to calm down,
The rain stopping the sun coming out,
There was a beautiful rainbow in the sky.

**Joshua Cornes (11)**
**Brewood CE Middle School**


# Da Croc

There was a croc that lived in the sewers
He eats
Toast and poached egg
Toast and butter
Toast and jam
Toast and marmalade
Toast and beans
Toast and everything

He grew from an egg
He grew in the sewers
His name was Little Mo
With the gimpy leg.

**Richard Harding (12)**
**Brewood CE Middle School**

# Bubbles

Bubbles are soft, bubbles are light
Bubbles are good for all eyesight
Bubbles tingle, bubbles ping
Bubbles are useful for everything

Bubbles don't harm you
Bubbles don't hurt
Bubbles pop when they land
On your shirt.

**Katie Morris  (11)**
**Brewood CE Middle School**


# The Ferry

It was a very dull day by the sea,
The waves crashing against the rocks,
On the edge of the cliff,
I saw the mist,
I saw the ferry go away.

The ferry, old and dusty,
Leaving rippling waves behind it,
I saw the ferry go away.

**Peter Timson  (11)**
**Brewood CE Middle School**


# The Snail On The Moon

The snail on the moon lives all alone,
Can you hear his wailing moan?
Slowly sliding across the surface,
Sliding at a very slow pace.
There's no gravity on the moon,
So that poor little snail will be dead very soon,
He needs to take shelter from the sun,
Or he'll end up like a currant bun.

**Katrina Haddon  (11)**
**Chesterton Community High School**

# Longing To Be Free

As the break of dawn rose up
There was a girl who longed so much to be free
From her puppet world
She would climb the highest mountains
Wishing she was a bird to fly high above the ocean
Longing so much to be free from her stringed world
She was getting old and rotting away
So she let go of all her dreams of ever being free
As the sun dropped down far beyond
She raised her arm to say one last goodbye
And then she was gone.

**Laura Reece  (12)**
**Chesterton Community High School**


# A Deer's Life!

Deer run for their lives,
Dodging bullets as they go,
*Bang!* All is quiet.

No places to run,
No hideout to discover,
Just running for miles.

From the beginning,
Mouths open wide whilst hounds run,
Chased to exhaustion.

**Alex Meakin  (12)**
**Chesterton Community High School**

# Fishing

F ine fish are good to eat
I f a very nice one, it might
S mile at you, it might not take the bait
H urt me and
I won't be very happy
N ow let's get some
G ood fish.

**Daniel Harley  (12)**
Chesterton Community High School


# Seven Deadly Sins

The first sin is lust,
For love you don't care,
For feelings you don't share.
The second sin is vanity,
For focussing on yourself,
For showing off your health.
The third sin is gluttony,
For the food you eat,
For the meals you repeat.
The fourth sin is wrath,
For anger you withhold,
For the pain that you mould.
The fifth sin is envy,
For how jealous you are,
For how your stares go far.
The sixth sin is greed,
For getting everything you want,
For knowing that you shouldn't.
The seventh sin is sloth,
For being oh so lazy,
For making yourself so hazy.
The seven deadly sins, you must beware,
The seven deadly sins, so do take care.

**Dominique Waller  (13)**
John Taylor High School

# Growing Up!

I want to grow up, Mum
I want to be big and tall
I'm the smallest in my family
Being little is no fun at all

I'm sick of being 3, Mum
It's really such a bore
Do you think if I ask Santa
He'll let me be four?

I need to be 13, Mum
I want to be a teen
Why can't I just be older?
You really are so mean

I need to be 16, Mum
So I can buy a home
You parents are too old for me
And just grumble and moan

Now I'm 34, Mum
And I have children too
I can see what you did for me
And I love you through and through!

I don't want to be 54, Mum
And see you dying now
I want us to be younger
I want you back but how?

I don't want to be 93, Mum
I don't want to die, I'm scared
I want to be back at 3, Mum
I don't think I'm prepared

I'm happy in your arms, Mum
Now everywhere is white
I feel like I am a child again
And you're kissing me goodnight.

**Bethany Lodge  (12)**
**John Taylor High School**

# Forest

One day in the forest, I went for a walk,
I listen to the birds as they squawk.
I can hear the trees swaying side to side,
They are so tall, so thick and so wide.
The rustling leaves form a blanket on the ground,
Some of them are oval and some of them are round.
The sun is shining brightly above the trees,
Then past my ear I feel a cool breeze.
I see a small squirrel run across the floor,
The wind picks up and begins to roar!
I hear the rain tapping on the leaves,
My boots get stuck so I must pull and heave.
A clap of thunder powers through the air,
A flash of light and I see some eyes stare.
I must run now or I will be drenched,
My boots get so stuck, I may need a wrench.
In the distance I see a small hut,
I go inside and slam the door shut.

**Richard George (12)**
**John Taylor High School**

# Winter Is Here

Snow is falling all around,
Jack Frost has come out to play.
Everything frozen in sight.
The roads too slippery and dangerous to drive.
Jack is in the middle of fun with his
Magic finger like a gun.
All the rivers and streams frozen,
All the fish sink to the bottom, stunned,
Snow still falling all around and trees dead with cold,
Jack still having fun with his gun.
Then spring is here, and Jack must go,
Because there will be sunshine and no more snow.

**William Rawbon (11)**
**John Taylor High School**

# The Dark

It's wrapping itself around me,
Closing in on me.
My eyes are not adjusted yet,
So nothing I can see.

The deep black lake of my covers,
There's nothing in my sight,
Only light from outside street lamps,
That are anything but bright!

In my sleep I can't hear noises
Or fear the creepy black,
Why don't I take that option?
Go to sleep now, don't look back.

There are too many shadows in corners
And too many sounds from outside
But what's that thing creeping up the stairs?
Help! Where shall I hide?

I squirm about in my covers
Squash up as tight as a ball
Surely the monster won't see me
If I'm tucked up nice and small.

But whose is that hand on my pillow?
Not a monster's claw for sure
It's as smooth as glass, like sand in my fingers
And I'm not scared anymore.

It's someone I know really well
It's someone who's playful and fun
It's someone who cares a lot about me
It's my mum!

**Hannah Lerigo (12)**
**John Taylor High School**

# Music Poem

Come take a look in my big music book;
If you get very near, who knows what you'll hear:

'I want you to leave,'
Said the fat semi-breve.
'What's got into him?'
Said the bossy minim.
'You'd better watch it,'
Said the angry young crotchet.
'What awful behaviour,'
Said the posh semi-quaver.
'We tried our best,'
Said the strong crotchet rest.
'Don't be so naughty!'
Said the fine, tall, loud forte.
'I can stand it no more,'
Said the mean five-lined score.

Things are not what they seem . . .
It has all been a dream!

**Tim Robinson (12)**
**John Taylor High School**

# Death

Why does it have to happen to me?
I thought it never would happen
Death is a harsh word
Sleep forever is much nicer
If you want to be wrapped up in cotton wool
There is nothing after death just darkness
Nothing only falling
Then white light all around
Nothing not even a sound
But is this true?
Will we ever find out?
We will find out when we're dead
But you can't tell anyone then
My time is coming soon
I'm expected to live till the next full moon
I would like to tell you about it
But I can't
My time has come
Goodbye.

**Claire Toman (12)**
**John Taylor High School**

# Homes

Houses sometimes come in pairs,
Like brand new shoes and matching socks.
There are battered houses where no one cares
And keys are lost to all the locks.

There are cottages all small and snug,
With roses arched around the door,
Vegetables are waiting to be dug
And rusty leaves scattered on the floor.

Vandalised flats are heaped up together,
Like playing cards, stacked up high,
Gangs are about, dressed in black leather
And a glint from a beggar's sad eye.

Grand mansions with their wrought iron gates,
The twisting drive goes round and round,
The balconies and fishing lakes,
With sweeping stairs that coil down.

**Gillian Panter (13)**
**John Taylor High School**


# In The Jungle

A drip of water cold and clear,
It's not the animals that I fear.
With tropical flowers, pink and red,
The trees whispering, I can hear in my head.
They swing through the trees, leaves rustle, twigs break,
Childish shouts and screams the monkeys make,
Distant buzzing of yellow and black bees,
Colourful birds sit and squawk in the trees.
Wet, sticky leaves wipe across my face,
Poisonous snakes move from place to place.
Blades of grass bend and sway,
The sun is high for the heat of the day.
Leopards sneak and lions creep,
Between the rocks the water seeps.

**Daniella Smith (12)**
**John Taylor High School**

# The Four Seasons

The four seasons come and go,
For what reason I do not know.
The spring beautiful, nice and calm
And there's the summer, hot like palm.

On the other hand there is winter,
Cold and sharp just like a splinter.
There's the autumn full of dew,
That is the season that some planes flew.

All of these seasons are unique,
They have their abilities and their leaks.
People like them, others don't,
The people bathe and others won't.

All of the seasons are amazing,
Why did God make this thing?

**Christopher Turner  (12)**
**John Taylor High School**


# I Love My Drums

I love playing my drum kit,
Crashing on the cymbals,
Making lots of noise,
The neighbours will complain,
But I don't really care.
I'll bash my drums all night and day,
Until my hands are sore.
Whether it's bashing on the floor tom,
Or smashing on the hi-hat,
I'll bash my drums all night and day,
Until my hands are sore.
Whether it's tapping on the ride,
Or knocking on the bass,
I'll bash my drums all night and day . . .
Until my hands . . . fall off.

**Peter Reisner  (12)**
**John Taylor High School**

# The Cat

For her eyes
She stole the twinkling of the stars,
She stole the green of the grass,
She stole the black of the night
And her eyes were made.

For her nose
She stole the wetness of the sea,
She stole the coldness of the snow,
She stole the healthiness of the fruit
And her nose was made.

For her teeth
She stole the sharpness of the ice,
She stole the whiteness of the milk,
She stole the thinness of the pin
And her teeth were made.

For her paws
She stole the softness of the clouds
She stole the roundness of the sun,
She stole the smallness of the stone
And her paws were made.

For her tail
She stole the longness of the snake,
She stole the fluffiness of the teddy,
She stole the wiggliness of the worm
And the tail was made.

The cat was made.

**Laura Nelson  (12)**
**John Taylor High School**

# Teddy's Bad Luck

The boxes are shoved onto the truck,
Oh how great, just my luck.
A teddy in a box, I'm on my way,
Pleasing kids is my job, mother's to pay.

We then arrived, the truck came to a halt,
Forcing my box to jump and jolt,
Next we were taken into a room,
Full of boxes, full of gloom.

Finally we were emptied onto a shelf,
But don't you worry, I was not by myself.
I was with hundreds of others, looking just like me,
No, I could spy new things to see.

The next morning I was sold,
I now have a person to cuddle and hold.
The girl takes me home,
When she's asleep, I have time to roam.

Now, years later, just look at me,
I have no eyes, I cannot see.
My nose is hanging by a thread,
I would much rather, just be dead.

The girl picks me up, years older now,
She stuffs me in a bag, but why, but how?
I know why, I know how,
I'm ruined, tatty and useless now.

So here I am, back in a truck,
But this time I have even less luck.
I'll be destroyed; I'm going to die,
I don't want to, I begin to cry.

**Grace Slights  (11)**
**John Taylor High School**

# Brothers And Sisters

My brother's a pain, they're all the same,
When I'm not looking, he gives me a squeeze,
Tickles my feet and squeezes my knees,
He trips me up and says, 'But, Mum!'
Messes my hair and gets a smack on the bum,
He thinks he's much bigger and better than me,
But I know better and far more than he.

A sister would be great; we could be best mates,
We could share our shoes, make-up and clothes,
Soak each other with water from the hose,
Go to the town and do things together.

But no because I have a brother,
Two will be OK and not such a bother,
We could all do things together and stick with each other
And when things go wrong we can be a family and play along.

**Hannah Slater  (13)**
**John Taylor High School**

# What Am I?

I swoop through the trees when nobody's there,
I fly like a white ghost, slicing the air.
My talons are like knives and they glint at the moon,
I glide, silent through its silvery shoon.
My cruel, cold beak slashes and cuts,
I eat only meat, no need for nuts.
I'm a nocturnal kite, looping the loop,
I look for my prey then I lash out and swoop.
I'm a danger to animals smaller than me,
I catch my prey then I fly for my tree.
I'm as small as a cat but I'll give you a scare,
I'm covered in feathers, they're softer than hair,
My friends come in grey or brown as a bear.
What am I?

**Katie Woods  (11)**
**John Taylor High School**

# Injustice

To see the anguish,
feel the bitterness,
it was too much.
With hurt and sorrow I turned away,
knowing I would never see it again,
only in my nightmares.

To think that he died for his causes,
his belief and even his humanity.
The only place I thought was right and just is not.

The smell of blood and flesh reeked all around,
people walking past the ground with not even the dignity or courage
to stop and look up, but just kept their heads down and kept walking,
that pained me to the soul.
But the core of the pain is the all knowing feeling
that it will happen sometime again.

**Lucy Moody (12)**
**John Taylor High School**


# Jungle

A silent rustle as something glides along,
Multicoloured flowers that smell and pong,
Succulent fruits hang from the trees,
Evil spiders hide in the leaves,
This is the place where the monkeys roam
And where waterfalls splash and foam.
Jaguars stalk their meal for the day,
Brightly coloured birds come out and play.
Snakes slither on the ground,
Looking for a bit of food to be found.
Creepers dangle out of the sky,
Mosquitoes all around they fly.
The sound of water dripping to the ground,
No cars or buses are to be found.

**Stuart Gale (12)**
**John Taylor High School**

# Yesterday

Thinking of yesterday, when you were still here
Thinking of yesterday brings me to tears
No one can help me, there's nothing to reduce the pain
Knowing I'll never see you smile again
My memories ruined, my dreams are crushed
Gone is my hero, who I loved so much
The world seems cold, the sky turns to grey
As I think of things I didn't get to say
Questions echo through my mind
Looking for an answer that I can't find

Years have passed and I've had time to deal with all the sorrow
No more longing for yesterday because all that matters is tomorrow
You have taught me a lesson like no one else has taught
And in a trap of sadness and regret I am no longer caught
For every time I see a star, I'll see the twinkle in your eye
And hear your voice when whispering wind sweeps through the sky
My dreams mean something if I want them to
And you are with me when I think of you
I can smile again if I let the memory of your presence
Live with me as a gift, not a loss every day
It's not an answer, just a way.

**Danielle Butler (13)**
**John Taylor High School**

# How Christmas Used To Be

A roaring fire, chestnuts roasting,
Joyful laughter from every door.
Merry hymns and magical wishes,
My brother and father safe back from the war.
That's what Christmas was all about,
That sparkle of joy in everyone's eyes.
Children's cheerful chirpish chatter,
A white woollen beard for Dad's disguise.

Seventy years on and alone here I lie,
My body has crumpled, my dignity's departed.
Minutes seem like hours as they crawl on by,
Hobbling as a retard where once I darted.

As I sit here remembering all alone,
The good times we shared bring warmth to my bones,
So remember you grasping, greedy gannets,
With your parents bustling and buying in panic.
Yuletide is about the shine of infants' smiles,
The sweet murmur of nativity prayers,
Not how high your presents pile.

I feel chilled with loneliness and old age as Advent slithers by,
I wish I had a family now laughing in merriment beside me.
Thinking how this precious time is ruined makes me cry
From greed and selfishness of Christmas today,
I wish I could break free.

**Sophie Hall  (13)**
**John Taylor High School**

# The School Bully

I stared into his big stony-grey eyes,
My head filled with dreading lies.
I felt the pain run though my chest,
He's never going to let me rest.

Horrible thoughts are running through my head,
I just want to hide underneath my bed.

Every time I walk past him,
He makes me feel so very dim.
He wants to meet me after school,
His mates think it is going to be cool.

Horrible thoughts are running through my head,
I just want to hide underneath my bed.

His red fists clench,
I'm just an innocent girl, sitting on a bench.
He's stomping, roaring, coming closer to me
And I'm just sitting, staring, waiting,
For the pain, the fear to enter me.

**Tanya O'Brien  (11)**
**John Taylor High School**

# Holidays

Waiting at the airport is what I hate
Especially when the flight is two hours late

When I got there, I looked around
And my missing suitcase is still not found

The next day, the sun goes in
And my new pair of glasses head for the bin

The good restaurants were full
And the one I went to was awful

I dropped my camera into the pool
I'm so embarrassed, I'm such a fool

I went to the pool, it was freezing cold
And full of green horrible mould

I went to the beach to see the sea
I was holding a sandwich and got stung by a bee

And now I am home and full of glee
Except for the washing, higher than me.

**Lauren Smith  (12)**
**John Taylor High School**

# My Dream World

In my dream world,
There is world peace.

In my dream world,
All wars will cease.

In my dream world,
The world is healthy.

In my dream world,
The poor are wealthy.

In my dream world,
There are people who care.

In my dream world,
There are people who share.

In my dream world,
Everyone is a friend.

In my dream world,
The world will never end.

**Sally Burton  (13)**
**John Taylor High School**

# Scared And Alone

Bombs, bombs, they are *madness*,
They scare everyone.
Everyone holds each other very tight,
When will they stop? *Who knows?*

Shaking, shaking, children are shaking,
They feel nervous and frightened.
They don't want to leave homes,
Crying, crying, they're flooding with fear.

They're big and white, they're cruel *labels*,
*Labels*, I have become a label,
I'm upset, worried.

Bleak, that's what the train station is,
It's cold, so very cold,
It's wet, very, very wet,
It's *frightening*.

The land is different to home,
Lots of green,
I'm scared and alone.

**Natasha Waller  (11)**
**John Taylor High School**

# Death By Skin

I'm suffocating in a pool of blood,
I'm drowning in a river of tears,
My body is covered in mud,
I feel like I have no ears,
You're suffocating my mind,
My freedom has freed itself from me,
You've got me in a bind,
Please just let me be,
What is all this for?
Why all the pain?
Why ask for more?
Are you really that insane?
Why all the mess?
Why can't you see?
Why am I less?
Is this what I had coming to me?
Just for the colour of my skin
And the way I talk
Or the country I live in?
I shall never be able to walk,
You've killed me, I am dead,
Everyone else will be too,
This is all for good you said,
But what does this really do?

**Lydia Hargrove  (14)**
**John Taylor High School**

# Treasure Hunt

The sea was raging
And the boat was ageing,
The waves grew tall,
Upon us they'd fall,
We knew it was time,
She'd reached the end of the line,
Above us it towered
And we became overpowered,
It came crashing down,
The water turned brown,
All was still,
After the kill,
Debris floated
And I felt bloated,
The water I swallowed,
Meant I was no longer hollowed,
Across the beach I lay,
Below the bright blue day,
Beside the lapping waves,
Next to the pitch-black caves,
Into the gloomy forest,
Beside the steep mount Morris,
Between the tall pine trees,
Through the wide bushy leaves,
In front of the island temple,
Beyond a pirate's reach,
Behind the village people,
I found the treasure chest.

**Hannah Dixon (13)**
**John Taylor High School**

# Thunder And Lightning

The animals
Huddle together
Under the trees
Now the rain is pouring
Down from the dark black sky
Entering through the tall dark trees
Rain finds its way through

Animals are frightened
Not knowing what's happening
Deafened by the cracks, crashes and flashes of

*Lightning*
It echoes through the darkness
Ground shakes as lightning strikes
How suddenly the power goes
The villages sit in darkness
No one can see
It clatters again
Now it is dying
Going into the night.

**Anna Meynell  (12)**
**John Taylor High School**

# The Same Old World

The cat, she prowls. The dog, he howls.
The robin, he tweets. The mouse, she squeaks.
They live together. They kill one another.
But live in the same old world.

The lion, he rules. Hyena, she drools.
Mosquito, she bites. Anteaters eat mites.
They sleep together. They live off each other.
And live in the same old world.

The parrot, she squawks. The vultures eat corpses.
The kangaroo leaps. The wolf, he eats sheep.
They play quite apart, but same in their heart.
Still live in the same old world.

Now people are thugs. They smoke and take drugs.
They drink and they drive. On killing they thrive.
If they were to look just over the brook,
They'd see stag and doe and soon they would know,
That they're killing our plentiful world.

**Doris Ward  (12)**
**John Taylor High School**

# Back To School!

Children arrive all clean and smart
Ready to begin a brand new start
Clean new books are given out
With no fuss or even a shout

Break time comes in a flash
Children run out in a dash
The queue for food is worth the wait
But hurry up otherwise you'll be late

Period three, time for maths
Learning about drawing graphs
Geography next with volcanoes galore
With the rippling lava and tremendous roar

In the classroom for registration.
Teachers screaming in frustration
'Jack and Tom, do not shout
You girls there, stop messing about!'

But that night when children go to bed
Lightning strikes through every head
The next day comes and with a groan
'I don't want to go to school, I want to stay at home!'

**Melissa Pomlett (11)**
**John Taylor High School**

# Absolutely Everybody

Look around you, look at the people,
Everyone you see, absolutely everybody is different.
Awkward children who won't make an effort,
Beautiful girls forever showing off.
Cheeky lads trying to look cool,
Destructive boys always causing trouble.
Excellent workers, the best in their class,
Friendly girls looking after the new kid.
Great friends always falling out,
Hard kids, the ones nobody messes with.
Intelligent boys stand watching the others play football,
Jealous girls planning their next stunt.
Kind children only trying to help,
Lazy lads, they just can't be bothered.
Model students, the ones we are supposed to look up to,
Nervous girls who just need a bit more confidence.
Popular lads who always have something to flaunt,
Quiet girls who don't want too much attention.
Rascally boys who never listen,
Sporty kids who try everything.
The misfit who nobody will talk to,
Ungrateful girls who don't really care.
Vain children who don't listen to others,
Wary boys watching their step.
But just because everyone is different,
Nobody deserves to be bullied.

**Torryn Kersey (11)**
**John Taylor High School**

# Fly With Me

Take yourself away today
High above the clouds
Into another dimension stray
Without time, without pollution

Come with me in my little machine
Look at the world another way around
Dive through candyfloss clouds
Soar above the toy town world and
Look at ant-like, multicolour and racing

Take yourself away today
Higher than an eagle
Come with me in my little machine
And off we will go on an adventure.

**George Clarke  (11)**
**John Taylor High School**


# Feeding Frenzy

The great white shark lurks in the sea,
Swimming swiftly through the water,
When he comes dashing through the water,
You think it cannot be.

You see a black shadow patrolling the sea,
When you see it in shallow water,
You shout to your innocent daughter,
You shout, 'Come back to me.'

But when you find out it is a great white,
Your daughter is nowhere in sight!

**Ryan Kavanagh  (12)**
**Maple Hayes Dyslexia School**

# Feeding Frenzy

Treacherous creature
Is the great white shark
It's worse than a teacher
Do something wrong, it's straight off the mark

They're fine until you enter their waters
Then they attack
A bump once, twice
Argh!

Swim, swim
Hurry, hurry
Help, help
Its huge jaws bite

Now you're in trouble
Blood everywhere
Hurry, hurry
Help, help
Too late, bye-bye to my life!

**Bruce Dale  (12)**
**Maple Hayes Dyslexia School**


# Lunchtime

Behind the cage you see the 8ft fish
Lurking around searching for his prey
I felt like I was going to die
Its big jaw, blood on its teeth
It lies on the bottom of the ocean
Waiting for his prey to jump in
Following his prey, waiting for the right time
The prey was then never seen again.

**Keyston Brown  (12)**
**Maple Hayes Dyslexia School**

# Going Down

When you see the boat
You wish it wasn't afloat
Teeth marks in the cage
You are starting to feel afraid
The engine is turned on
Your stomach does churn
Shark attacks happen
Crew members have scars
I look at some big crowbars
I am having second thoughts
I put my wetsuit on me
Bite marks near the knee
Meat is being put in the sea
Grey fins are appearing.

**Daniel Garner (12)**
**Maple Hayes Dyslexia School**


# I Feel Like Human Tonight

His big white bloody teeth
The dorsalled fin coming like a missile
You don't know what it is

You don't know it is in
Until it bites and you have one leg

You can't get away
When you are face to face
You might as well obey.

**Charles Carden (12)**
**Maple Hayes Dyslexia School**

# Babies!

A screaming sound that throbs and pounds
Night and day
I don't think I could live this way
A sweet, fresh smell spreads through the house
Creeping around like a mouse
'It's a boy,' they shout
You pick him up again and you'll have a clout
Hold him, just for a min
Put that nappy sack in the bin
Nag, nag, nag
Brag, brag, brag
That's all I ever do for you
I am a slave for you
Wait until you have a baby
What? OK, maybe.

**Hayley Turner  (13)**
**Painsley Catholic High School**


# Haunted House

Are you a man or a mouse?
Come along to the haunted house,
We'll give you a fright
And send you screaming into the night.
There are goblins and ghouls,
Old witches cackling in worn black cagoules,
As for your host,
Well, he is a ghost,
Come to the haunted house,
Are you a man or a mouse?

**Matthew Rowley  (14)**
**Painsley Catholic High School**

# Love

Love is a mystery,
That has been there for all of history,
Some may think that love is to cherish,
Others say that it makes us perish.
Love can make us fly,
Up high in the sky,
Although it may seem,
That love is a dream,
It is real,
As it can make us feel,
Love is one's desire,
That may light their fire,
Love can start with a date,
Then the rest is fate,
Love is so gentle,
It can make us go mental,
Love can't be found in a charm or a potion,
It seems that it is just a notion,
Love may be at first sight,
If it is, then it's a delight,
Love can be scary,
Like a monster that's hairy,
Or love can be fun,
Like playing in the sun.

**Paul Dudley  (14)**
**Painsley Catholic High School**


# Family

Happy and joyful, my mum towards me,
My father full of good humour and glee,
My sister's never in for me to see,
No attention paid toward me,
Sitting up in my room,
Wishing they would come and see me soon.

**Danielle Hill  (14)**
**Painsley Catholic High School**

# Titanic

Titanic was the ship of dreams,
The queen of the ocean or so it seemed.
The great white sparkle from the ship glowed with shine,
As first class people sipped their wine.

The luxurious ship sailed the sea,
The days on total were only three,
For on the 4$^{th}$ night there was a sudden fright,
An iceberg right ahead.

The Titanic hit with a thundering crash, huge smash,
As lower decks started to flood,
The crew lost control and there was loss of blood.
Lifeboats started to sail but there was by far not enough,
Many men jumped to their death and were engulfed.

Early the next morning 2.20am,
The Titanic plunged into the freezing sea.
To start with, the sea was full of poor people,
But by the end of the night, only 6 poor souls had survived.

**Katie Finney  (14)**
**Painsley Catholic High School**


# Family

My family argue day and night,
They never know when to stop,
Scared and lonely like I'm to blame,
Locked in my room like a lion trapped in a cage.
My dad hitting and shouting at my mum,
My mum screaming stop at him with fear.
I can hear smashes and bangs downstairs
And I wonder if someone is hurt!
Too afraid to go downstairs in case I get hurt.
I just sit here with my dog in my room,
Praying it will be over soon.

**Kirsty Dunn  (14)**
**Painsley Catholic High School**

# Immersion . . .

I want to live,
I want to be me,
I want to feel myself run and just be free.

Run through the mountains of snow and rock,
For in this daily life I cannot.

I long to be immersed in the deepest snow,
Somewhere, miles from any foe.

I want to be surrounded by friends,
Until the deep, cold days, until the Earth ends.

I want to breathe,
I want to feel the blood rushing through my veins.

Then I can live,
Then I can be free,
Only then can I be immersed in me.

**Ross Daniels (14)**
**Painsley Catholic High School**


# Loneliness

I was all on my own, no one to talk to, no one to see,
I had a loathsome feeling inside me!
What was it? I do not know,
Could it be me or could it just be you?
As the floors began to creak, I felt myself begin to peak,
Out of the window I did stare,
To see such a happy pair,
Down the road they did walk,
How I wished I was like that,
Just to blow away this lonely feeling!

**Laura Mycock (14)**
**Painsley Catholic High School**

# All Alone

It's Christmas Day, the bells are ringing
Children are singing
Snowflakes are falling
The roads are appalling
I stand in a room alone and forgotten
There are no presents and the room is all rotten
My mum and dad were ever so crude
Said I swore a lot and was rude
I miss them, the way they used to moan
That would mean I wouldn't be alone
I walk out onto the street
I feel all hot and my heart starts to beat
I see my next-door neighbour showing off her new clothes
The only thing she does to me is look down her nose
I wish I could go home
Then I wouldn't be alone.

**Charlotte Ashby (13)**
**Painsley Catholic High School**


# Confusion

No more hatred, no more fear,
No more waiting until anger will appear.
I'm running fast, no matter where,
I can't go back, I hate it there.
My hair blows from side to side,
I'm lonely, I feel hurt inside.
I reach the cliff where my destiny lies,
My mother screams, my family cries.
Why don't I end my life here?
My mother soon approaches near.
She grips my hand, now I'm not alone,
She holds me tight and takes me home.

**Elizabeth Lasota (14)**
**Painsley Catholic High School**

# Homework . . .

Teachers like to nag,
Moaning all the time,
Shouting at you for not doing homework,
As if it's some sort of crime.

Keeping you in at break,
Giving you a 1000 lines,
Teachers like to nag,
Moaning all the time.

Teachers like to nag,
Moaning all the time,
Doing their best to detain you,
For wasting some of their time.

Keeping you in at dinner,
Sanding down the desks,
Teachers like to nag,
That's what they do best.

**Steven Baddeley  (14)**
**Painsley Catholic High School**


# Alone I Am

Alone I am
Alone is a word everyone fears
Alone is what I am
Alone is bad
Alone is sad
Alone is enough to turn one mad

Alone I am
Alone is making me cry
Alone with no one passing by
Alone is my life
Alone I am.

**Nicholas Harvey  (14)**
**Painsley Catholic High School**

# Bullying

Run, run, that's all I can do,
He's gaining, he's gaining, what can I do?
He's getting closer and closer.
Faster and faster,
Bang . . . I fall to the ground as fast as a bullet.
His fat fingers as long as forks,
Fell upon my face.
I'm dead, I'm dying, I think in dismay.
The beating is brutal, as hard as a brick,
I have to bite down upon my lip.
Then he stops . . . only to start all over again.
I can feel his hands piercing my skin,
As hard as a pin,
Then to my rescue an adult has come to save.

**David Daniels  (13)**
**Painsley Catholic High School**


# Family

This is one thing you cannot live without,
They sometimes argue and maybe even shout.
They send you to your room, strongly with no care,
But even though they banish me, the love is still there.
I go down to say I'm sorry, then they embrace me,
We all get over our arguments and settle down to tea,
We relish as we eat and chat about our day.
They have smiles on their faces and everything seems OK,
Until my dad comes in drunk again and beats up my mum.
Whilst my little sister watches, sucking on her thumb.
Tears run down my cheek, what has my dad become?
The bruises will fade but I know that it will happen again.

**Luke Daly  (14)**
**Painsley Catholic High School**

# Thinking Of Someone Special

Thinking of you as the days go by
Sitting at home all by myself
Thinking of all the good moments we shared
Only to realise that you're gone

I know that time heals
Yet I want this pain to go away
I know my love is safe
Yet mystery and romance appear to me
I know that life sometimes can be a chore
But what my heart wants from you is so much more

I know that there is safety in numbers
Yet I long to be alone
There are some moments which I want to last forever
Yet I know that change is inevitable
I know friendships sometimes end
Yet I need a friend right to the end

I know people must move on
Yet we part to meet
I know the tune of many songs
Yet I desire the word to move on

I know all these things
Yet I want so much more
Sometimes in life, we remain where we are
Because it's what we know best
But is it really what we want?

**Kamurai Wabatagore (13)**
**Painsley Catholic High School**

# The Final Leap

Riding slowly to the woods,
The tension gradually builds up,
The race is about to start,
I know by the thudding of my heart,
Someone shouts, 'Go,'
Now it's time to start,
Everyone chooses a different route,
Each trail is littered with different obstacles,
It would be a work of miracles,
If I won now,
I lost lots of speed,
As I hit an overgrown weed,
Swerving through the trees,
The finish was in my sights,
When Chris appeared from the right,
The choice was clear,
Jump with no fear,
Flying through the air,
I'm so very nearly there,
Photo finish - Chris or me,
The scoreboard flashes - I can't see,
Because everyone is congratulating me.

**Matthew Capper  (14)**
**Painsley Catholic High School**

# The Pond

The sun glistened across the pond
Reflecting the trees and sound of birds in song
The peace is broken by the sound of geese in flight
Their wings spread the smoothness of a kite
As they roost up on a frosty, friendly, old oak tree
One, two, three, it doesn't matter when they are free.

**Matthew Prince  (14)**
**Painsley Catholic High School**

# As Long As It Takes

To never realise what you put me through
It's not hard to show how much I care
The only thing I dream of
This hurtful pain I have to bare
The memories of all my life
Always and forever haunt me
The winter comes, the warmth is gone
Like leaves that fall from a wilting tree
The joy in your eyes
The smile in my heart
A racing pulse
To be never apart
Sitting, watching every day
I hoped you still looked my way
You glance around and see me stare
But turn away without a care
I notice she is looking too
It's obvious she's in love with you
Tears that hurt, I begin to cry
Slowly you are slipping by
I had you once, once before
No happiness now, forever more
One chance I had, but let it go
If I walk away, you'll never know
You are gone
But still I wait
The scars run deep
Though I cannot hate.

**Natasha Hallam  (14)**
**Painsley Catholic High School**

# Romeo And Juliet

At the Capulet ball,
Romeo did fall
In deep desire of Juliet.
Tybalt already knew,
Romeo was a Montague,
So wanted to see him dead.
In the dead of night,
To Juliet's delight,
Romeo came back to her house.
The very next day,
They went away
And got married in the church.
A brawl in the street,
Lead to Mercutio's decease,
While Tybalt was the victor.
At this sight,
Romeo did fight
And Tybalt was no longer.
To Prince Escalus' disgrace,
Benvolio pleaded Romeo's case,
So Romeo's life was spared.
Instead he got banished,
After midnight he vanished,
Much to Juliet's horror.
She took a potion,
Which cut off her motion
And put her in a deep sleep.
At each other's deaths,
Romeo and Juliet took their last breaths,
So their family feud was over.

**Rebecca Heron  (14)**
**Painsley Catholic High School**

# Weather

Blustery days and the wind bawling at night,
Murky by five so not much in sight.
Lengthy dark months that we have to endure,
That's winter for you, that's for sure.
Leaves swirling around our feet,
Our pleasurable gardens now don't look so neat.
Frost in the morning and last thing at night,
Makes everywhere you look so sparkling white.
I rouse to the vision of pure white snow,
In our heated homes there is a enchanting glow.
Children laughing and racing around outside,
Constructing snowmen and sledging, 'Hey, let me have a ride.'
Then we have rain plummeting through the sky,
Belting down on the ground which was previously dry.
Occasionally it's hail, leaping up and down,
'Quick' let's go back indoors, before we drown.
'Oh' I dream of the sun and the warm, placid breeze,
To eliminate my cold and my sneeze and wheeze.
To rest on a beach, where the sun smoulders my skin,
Just like a cat on a hot roof tin,
Changing our skin tone to brown or red,
'Plenty of suncream on,' is what Mum said.
Tanned, radiant skin, beneath the starry sky,
Sipping at my drink, I let out a huge sigh;
Nothing stays the same forever,
Things change all the time just like the weather.

**Kayleigh Allen (14)**
**Painsley Catholic High School**

# Many Types Of Friends

There are many types of friends
How can we choose?
Many we gain and some we love
How you perceive them, it all depends

There are many types of friends
Fat ones, thin ones
Tall ones, small ones
Blond-haired friends and brown-haired friends
Eyes which are beautiful blue or guarded green
How you perceive them, it all depends

There are many types of friends
You get to know along the way
The ones you don't like will only last a day
How you perceive them, it all depends

There are many types of friends
Confident or shy
Giggly or calm
Lovely and loud, quiet and secretive
Daring and dangerous or cowardly and safe
How you perceive them it all depends

There are many types of friends
I hope that you will find
Your special friend that you have in your mind

There are many types of friends
I hope that you will find
Your special friend that you have in your mind
How *you* perceive them is the only thing that depends!

**Lauren Tilstone  (14)**
**Painsley Catholic High School**

# Sinking Poem

Slowly descending
Into the deep blue sea
Frightened is the feeling
Deep inside of me

Panicking and shaking
Tremors in my heart
All my body aching
Tearing me apart

Down and down, my body goes
Wrestling with my soaking clothes
Hold my breath, my chest all tight
Trying to swim is such a fight

The water's swirling around my head
This terrible feeling is what I dread
My body's weak as cold as ice
I swallowed water, that was not nice

Can someone save me? Is all I ask
Of course I see that's an impossible task
The water's got me, it's all too late
Now I know this is my fate.

**Natalie Wolff  (14)**
**Painsley Catholic High School**


# Confusion

I drift down the stairs,
What will today bring?
At the present time it is spring,
My father is happy,
But my mother is sad,
For I must of done something really bad.
I can't work it out!
Because my father is happy,
But my mother is sad.

**Ben Stott  (14)**
**Painsley Catholic High School**

# My First Day At School

Honk, honk,
Here comes the bus,
Butterflies in my stomach,
What a fuss.

The trees tower over,
Casting a shadow,
I walked on into my fear,
There are children of all ages,
Some big, some small,
Running around and kicking a ball.

They run past shouting out loud,
Almost deafening, a horrific sound.
Clang clang, goes the bell,
Time to face my fiery hell.

I walk inside, I feel blind,
Not knowing where to go
Or what to do.

It is worse than my nightmares,
Only this was real.

**Robbi Hill  (13)**
**Painsley Catholic High School**


# We're On The Ball

G loves on to grip the ball
O ur studs on so we don't fall
A ll his own, he's number one
L eft or right, where has the ball gone?
K eep alert, don't let a goal in
E very fan wants us to win
E ach player has half-time rest
P enalty – oh no! I'll do my best
E veryone's hero if I save it
R eserves bench if I fail.

**Jamie Capper  (11)**
**Painsley Catholic High School**

# So You Might Ask!

It's back again,
What? you might ask.
You know, that horrible, earth-shattering
Marriage-splitting thing,
So? you might ask.
Those soaking wet, muddy trenches,
The horrendous, ear-splitting noises of
Tanks, bombs and constant gunfire.
So? you might ask.
The dead, the POWs,
Seeing your best friend dead,
You know what it is, it's *war!*

I can't believe my eyes,
I signed up again.
I wish I'd never contemplated this,
I ran forward with my gun blazing rapidly,
The fear of death surrounded me.
So? you might ask.
This is worse than before,
I hear soldiers from my platoon
Scream in anguish as they are shot at.
So? you might ask.
I step over the dead bodies
And listen to the bombs being dropped.
So? you might ask.

**Adam Atkinson (13)**
**Painsley Catholic High School**

# The Dragon

There was once a dragon
Who couldn't breathe fire
He was laughed at by the others
And he was not to admire

He had no friends
And was all alone
He was bullied by the others
And he was never allowed to moan

He was a small dragon, everybody said
'You would never make a proper dragon'
For he would never prosper

But one day while he was alone
Sitting and sobbing
He stood up suddenly
And started coughing

He suddenly let off a huge burst of fire
And everyone came rushing
They all stared at him
As he was blushing

There was once a happy dragon
Who could breathe fire
He laughed with his friends
And he was to admire.

**Jorge Lindley (13)**
**Painsley Catholic High School**

# My First Day At School

I couldn't bear those chains,
Opening on the gates,
It made it look like a prison,
With those rusty gates.

I walked inside onto the school yard,
There I was all alone,
Standing in one spot,
People would shove past me,
Like I was unseen.

When I went to my lesson,
I did loads of work,
People said I was a teacher's pet,
Doing all of the work that was set.

When it was home time,
I couldn't wait to hear the bell,
I would rush to the bus park,
To get away from my nightmares in Hell.

**Charlotte Gumny (13)**
**Painsley Catholic High School**

# Haikus

Along comes the spring
All the flower buds open
And grass is growing

Summer is now here
The weather is very hot
So some people swim

Autumn has arrived
All the leaves fall off the trees
They rustle and crunch

Winter is now here
Hedgehogs go and hibernate
Children on their sledge.

**Amy Whitehurst (11)**
**Painsley Catholic High School**

# My Dinosaur Ate My Dog

A dinosaur ate my dog last night.
The nasty thing, it only took one bite!
It crushed her in its steel vice,
The nasty thing, that wasn't nice.

Blood and guts went everywhere,
But all Dad could do was stand and stare.
A dinosaur ate poor Shelly
And now she's in its belly.

A dinosaur ate my dog last night.
It was not a pretty sight!
A dinosaur ate my little pet,
Now no one can save her, not even the vet.

My dog got eaten last night by the way!
Or so, that's what my parents say.
I've had her since I was seven,
Now she's up in doggy heaven.

A dinosaur ate my dog last night.

**Martin Bland  (14)**
**Painsley Catholic High School**


# A Dream

When the sun shines down on me,
The birds are singing in the trees.
The neighbours wave hello and goodbye
And in the trees the squirrels play and hide.
A perfect world this would be,
If it was not just a dream,
A dream I have every night,
A dream that doesn't fill me with fright.
The children play, smile and have fun,
All beneath the big yellow sun.
A perfect world this would be,
If it was not just a dream.

**Natasha Ekin  (14)**
**Painsley Catholic High School**

# United In The Universe

A black canvas
Cascaded with drops of dust
Fills the sky at night
And when I look above the heavens
My troubles seem to be there
And central to the shiny stars
Is the man inside the moon
And no matter the troubles of the world
He still remains the same
I know that people are looking at the moon
Just the same as me
From all the walks of life
But that's what makes us all united
The sun, the moon, the stars
So next time you look to the man upon the night
Remember your brothers and sisters
Are there with you tonight.

**Lucy Wrightson (14)**
**Painsley Catholic High School**

# Bullying!

B ullying happens almost everywhere in the entire world
and it should not be tolerated.

U nder no circumstances should you bully someone,
it's not fair and it makes people feel really awful and worthless.

L earn to tolerate someone who you don't like, even if it means
not going near them at all.

L ike the people who are around you and respect them.

Y ou should not bully someone who is different to you,
everyone deserves respect.

I t is not a good thing to bully someone, it's a bad thing.

N obody is to be bullied, it's not fair, it causes people to
be unhappy and depressed.

G roups of bullies are even worse than one bully.

**Patrick Floyd (14)**
**Painsley Catholic High School**

# Fear

In my house all alone,
I feel so small, I try to hide.
I am not scared,
OK, I am scared.
Oh no, I cannot bear,
What's over there?
Will it give me a scare?
Am I going to die?
I think it's coming closer,
Is it a friend?
We will find out now,
My heart is racing,
'Come on out,' I shout,
But there's nothing there.
There's nothing there!
With all my fear and guts of pride,
I look to see who is there.
It's . . . it's my dad,
He won't give me a scare.
My fear has gone,
I'm not on my own.
I'm not on my own!

**Chris Moult  (13)**
**Painsley Catholic High School**


# Fear

My family argue day and night,
I sit and watch the stars in the sky,
As I hear Mum's screams, I wish I could fly to my dreams,
Where I shall be queen and happy are those who are full of care.
Then as I realise I'm not quite there,
All I can hear is smashes and bangs,
But I'm too scared to go down,
I feel alone, no one to hug me and no one to love me,
I close my eyes and wonder what I shall find in the morning.

**Natalie Hudson  (14)**
**Painsley Catholic High School**

# My Brother

My brother is my best friend,
He's a very funny lad.
He always sticks up for me,
When I'm in trouble with my dad.

He helps me with my homework,
When I don't know what to do
And when my mum and dad go out,
He looks after me too.

I am proud to be his sister,
He is extremely clever.
Would I want to change him?
No way, never!

Now my brother has gone to uni,
I miss him very much,
But I will see him very soon
And we will never lose touch.

**Laura Simpson  (14)**
**Painsley Catholic High School**


# Bullying Is . . .

Bullying is when the room goes cold
as the bullies target their next victim

Bullying is when you hear a cold threatening
voice whispered in your ear

Bullying is when you are alone
and don't feel that you are noticed

Bullying is a nasty, bitter feeling

Bullying is a horrible, selfish thing to do

Bullying is a thing sometimes caused by
their bullies being threatened by their victim

Bullying is *not* wanted in this poem.

**Emma Lawton  (13)**
**Painsley Catholic High School**

# Never Say Never

When we met, right at the start,
That first time I saw you, you were grasped by my heart.
Then I left, without saying goodbye,
That spark will melt down, burn out and die.

Although I think of you, every day that goes by,
It's hard to imagine you not being in my life.
I was told when I left, that I'd never return,
To that beautiful paradise, so instead I shall yearn.

What are you doing? Who are you with?
Living in wonder, is how I now live.
Do you know I have gone? Do you remember my face
Or have you forgotten? Is that the case?

If you realised I'd gone, without a trace,
You knew I'd never come back, that was the case,
But never say never, I've made up my mind,
Some day in the future, I'll leave England behind.

**Sarah Rushton  (14)**
**Painsley Catholic High School**


# The Graveyard

Cold, wet night; I peer through the bars,
The graveyard glistens beneath the stars.

Gravestones are scattered all around,
The mist lifts slowly off the ground.

The eerie silence is quickly broken,
By a hidden owl? No, the dead are awoken.

The bats sweep to and fro,
I push the rusting gates and in I go.

Along the path, I slowly creep,
Trying not to disturb them from their sleep.

Who is watching? Who is there?
All I do is stand and stare.

**Hayley Fearn  (13)**
**Painsley Catholic High School**

# Lonesomeness

Left in the world alone,
No friends to comfort me,
About me they moan,
They leave me with no glee.

They leave me completely friendless,
I am left without care,
My whole life is a big mess,
I'm ready to lose my hair.

I am dwelling in my own world,
Left in isolation,
In my ball I am curled,
I am in desolation.

No one to cheer me up,
No one to help me,
They walk by and spit in my cup,
Why don't they just kill me?

I want this all to just end,
I really hate my life,
It's going to drive me round the bend,
Life's constantly great strife.

**Alexander Humphreys  (14)**
**Painsley Catholic High School**

# Water

The water runs smoothly down the rocks,
Crashing gently on the docks,
Sleek and shiny; blue and white,
The small stream reflects the light.
A boy wanders through the stream,
As if entranced by a dream.
The rocks gently torn apart,
With tranquillity passes a silent cart.

**Luke Bath  (13)**
**Painsley Catholic High School**

# National Poetry Day . . .

We stand lined up outside the door
Waiting for English, what a bore!
The teacher arrives with a smile on her face
'In you go, proceed with grace'

We all sit down and look around
No one dared make a sound
Then the teacher stood up to say
'Cheer up, it's National Poetry Day'

My heart began to race faster
As I realised the task to master
I sat, staring at the sheet
Thinking of how to tackle the feat

At last I struck upon an idea
To write a poem about my fear
The fear of National Poetry Day
But what was I going to say?

I began to write about the chore
Which the whole class found a bore
I took a glance at the sheet
And realised I'd accomplished my feat.

**Victoria Lamburn  (13)**
**Painsley Catholic High School**


# We Know Who You Are

We all know who you are
So give yourself up
And we'll leave you in peace
Just shut your mouth up

We all know you're a robber
Who is not a very nice man
So please would you do us a favour
And give that man back his van.

**Kate Buttress  (12)**
**Painsley Catholic High School**

# The Teacher

You son, yes son, you son.
What do you think you're doing?
Two minutes of my time wasted,
Maybe I should waste two minutes of yours.
You wouldn't catch people in the army behaving like that,
You've got to be vigilant, you're in the school army now.

You son, yes son, you son.
I'll be reasonable and ask you nicely to tuck your shirt in.
No tuck it in, don't roll it.
I don't know if you can be trusted to keep that in.
Even though you've got enough freedom at home,
Don't let me catch you again.

You son, yes son, you son.
Where's your homework?
I asked for your asthma homework twelve weeks ago, where is it?
What? You still haven't got it?
You've been on holiday have you? Well it's all right for some
people isn't it?

Well, I expect 100 lines for tomorrow
On why you should bring your homework.

**Philip Long  (14)**
**Painsley Catholic High School**


# Hallowe'en

H allowe'en is scary
A llowing the pumpkins
L aughter is not but scares are a
L ot
O h what can we do because we can't thank you
W e are scared to death
E ven at bedtime at
E ight o'clock the terrors will all stop
N ow it is all galore.

**Andrew Williamson  (13)**
**Painsley Catholic High School**

# Class One Chaos Hell

The little monsters smile at her, it's nine o'clock again,
'Come on Sarah, sit down Laura, please don't fidget Ben!
Now, today we'll do some colouring . . .' the little faces smile.
'. . . Or if you want, some painting, haven't done that for a while.'
She reaches for the brushes, the paint and paper too,
Then over to the cupboard for the crayons and the glue.
She puts them on the table and their little hands dig in
And in a moment, it's not long before the stress begins.
She turns her head to see the class and finds a shocking sight,
Jimmy's sleeves are in the paint, all colourful and bright.
The quiet ones are just as bad, Jenny's speckled blue.
Simon's eating crayons and Charlotte's in the glue.
Caroline trips over and the paint splats on the floor
And Katie grins contentedly as she scribbles on the door.
A purple coloured crayon is lodged in Phillip's nose
And he's hitting little Matty, halfway through his doze.
The chaos halts suddenly at the ringing of the bell,
Behind them is the aftermath of class one's chaos hell.

**Oonagh Scannell (14)**
**Painsley Catholic High School**


# Monday Morning

I open my eyes, daylight I see,
Waking up on Monday mornings, there's nothing worse for me,
I bury my head under the pillow,
It's Monday morning, to school I have to go,
I clamber out of bed and wrestle my trousers on,
'Hurry up!' shouts Dad. 'Are you ready, Son?'
I stagger around the kitchen to find the Shredded Wheat,
I glance towards the clock, the bus I have to meet,
I go into the bathroom to give my teeth a brush,
The bus is on its way, I really need to rush,
Off I go to catch the bus, the shelter has a leak,
That is Monday morning, the beginning of the week.

**Joseph Earley (14)**
**Painsley Catholic High School**

# Drumming

Drumming is one of my favourite things,
The crashes of cymbals, the rings and the dings.
I smash my sticks on the rim,
My mum shouts from upstairs, 'Stop making a din!'
I love the colour of them, wine-red
And still my mum shouts, 'You'll wake the dead!'

Even though all my drums have a dampener pad,
It still manages to drive my mum mad!
I'm sure when I get better and it's not so loud,
My mum will of course be proud!
When I'm older I'll start a band,
We'll be that famous we'll be on demand!

Dum, dom, dum,
My hands have gone numb.
Should I stop?
Soon my arms will drop,
But I'm having so much fun,
Now my feet weigh a ton!

Drumming is really ace,
But you have to have a quick pace.

**Mark Deighton  (14)**
**Painsley Catholic High School**

# Mothers And Fathers

Mothers and fathers
help us all the time.
Mothers and fathers
help us write on the lines.

Mothers and fathers
tell us off.
Mothers and fathers
pat us on the back when we cough.

Mothers and fathers
take us to school.
Mothers and fathers
let us play in the paddling pool.

Mothers and fathers
tuck us up in bed at night.
Mothers and fathers
let us switch on the light.

Mothers and fathers,
we care about them.
Mothers and fathers,
but best of all we *love* them.

**Charlotte Priddey  (13)**
**Painsley Catholic High School**

# A Loved One

It's like the thundering crashing
Of an icy cold waterfall
It's hard to believe
When they're happy, they leave

It's like the deadly silence
Which comes with nightfall
I can't understand
You were so close to hand

It's like discordant music
Played loud like a caterwaul
Inescapable
And inevitable

It's like a scream in the darkness
Echoing against the wall
Cold, unexpected
Thought I'd be unaffected

It's like a piercing pain
Relieved by no drug
Broken heart, broken wing
Death, it's an evil thing.

**Hannah Mycock  (14)**
**Painsley Catholic High School**


# Ghosts

G hosts go wherever they please
H ouse by house
O n winter days they haunt graveyards
S itting, waiting to haunt
T errifying their victims
S ticking to a victim until it dies.

**Nicolas Shaw  (12)**
**Painsley Catholic High School**

# Raining And Raining

Raining hard, never stopping,
Mums take cover with their shopping.
Black clouds rolling way up high,
Scattering droplets fall from the sky.

Raining fast, keeps on coming,
On the windows it's drumming.
Thunder rolls and lightning strikes,
Why won't this rain just take a hike?

Raining down, hear it pattering,
Pattering and splattering.
Falling into many puddles,
Oh how this weather is in a muddle.

Raining loudly, it never shuts up,
Oh how the sun must be fed up.
We never see it anymore,
Just keeps on raining like before.

Splish, splosh, splash, it just won't go away,
Keeps on going night and day,
Raining and raining.

**Harriet Collier  (12)**
**Painsley Catholic High School**


# The Sea

The sun cast its shadow over the clear blue sea,
The golden beach lay before my feet.
The waves at the sea came crashing at me,
The seagulls skimmed across the sea,
This is where I want to be!

The sky became dark and the moon came out,
The stars shone bright in the deep, deep sky.
The waves smashed fiercely against the coast,
The tide came in and dragged my thoughts out to sea.
This is where I want to be!

**Thomas Arme  (13)**
**Painsley Catholic High School**

# Autumn

Bright summer skies are fading,
Dark clouds are drawing near,
Forests are a blaze of colour,
Winds are full of fear.

The leaves are falling from the trees,
Fluttering in the air,
Red berries in the mist appear,
Shorter days are very near.

Rain beating on our window panes,
Leaves blowing all around,
Falling piles
Of orange, gold and brown.

Pumpkins in the fields,
Gold above the ground,
Hallowe'en around the corner,
A full moon lights the town.

Out come the long-sleeved sweaters,
Blankets on the bed,
Cold nights are drawing near,
With long dark nights ahead.

The squirrels are busy harvesting
And the birds in flight appear,
Now we know for certain,
Autumn is really here.

**Matthew Forrester (11)**
**Painsley Catholic High School**

# Hallowe'en

There isn't another night like Hallowe'en,
Where all the ghosts and ghouls are seen,
This is a night when you dress up and go trick or treating,
But you never know what you are greeting.

On this night the moon shines bright,
The stars twinkle and shimmer all night,
You look up and see a witch swoop by,
On her broomstick as fast as she can fly.

When you look up again she has flown away,
But will she come back on another day?
Her hair was like a bird's nest,
She obviously hadn't tried her very best.

You look back down at the ground
And see your friends are not around,
You look around and cannot see,
That all your friends are nowhere to be.

Walking up a big steep hill,
Everything stood silent and still,
Then you go in your house,
Everyone's as silent as a mouse.

Stepped into the kitchen, 'Mum, I'm back.'
She said to you, 'What have you in that sack?'
It got tipped out and all you saw,
Was loads of candy on the floor.

All your family grabbed a sweet
And they got ready to eat,
On the clock it was nearly half-ten,
Mum said, 'Go up to bed' and you said, 'When?'

Mum said, 'Now', so you went up to sleep,
You thought about all the candy you could keep,
You dreamt about the night you like,
It's Hallowe'en, it gives you a fright.

**Marie Insley (13)**
**Painsley Catholic High School**

# I Feel

Sometimes I feel like . . .
Hitting a hare,
Punching a parrot,
Shooting a snail,
Beating a bear,
Strangling a snake,
Frightening a frog,
Maiming a mouse,
Firing on a fox,
Exploding an earwig,
Stamping on a slug,
Killing a kangaroo,
Electrocuting an elephant,
But actually I wouldn't do any of that,
Because I would rather stroke my cat,
But that doesn't rhyme, so that's that!

**Tom Bland  (11)**
**Painsley Catholic High School**


# Christmas

As the winter begins to dawn,
Shivers can be found at morn,
Whispers lost in the icy mist,
As children write their Christmas list.

Snowflakes fall into the snow,
Far in the distance lights gleam and glow,
The tender sparkle of a child's eye,
Warms the heart and a tear I cry.

Cries of laughter, cries of glee,
Presents neatly wrapped beneath the tree,
For Christmas is a time I know,
For people to love and their love to show.

**Lucy Offen  (13)**
**Painsley Catholic High School**

# Three Idiot Pirates On A Washing Line

One day on a pirate ship,
When all was very quiet,
Captain Podge woke suddenly
To the sound of a riot.
So he walked up onto the deck,
In a very, very bad mood
And before his eyes, he saw his crew
Throwing what was left of the food.
'I've had enough!' he shouted,
'I've had enough!' he yelled.
There were fish heads on the floor
And the whole ship smelt.
He took the three of them by their pants
And hung them on the washing line
And whilst they got bad wedgies,
Captain Podge sipped wine.
The next day, he woke to find that his human hoard
Had slipped silently, oh so quietly, slowly overboard.

**Alexandra Foulkes  (11)**
**Painsley Catholic High School**


# Spring

Spring has sprung, it's all begun,
The birds have come to sing their songs.
Spring has sprung, it has all come back,
Animals wake from their long hibernation.
Spring has sprung just like before,
The flowers have come back to life and have coloured our fields.
Spring has sprung and so has life,
The sun has come so we are warm.
Spring has sprung just like Christ,
Easter has arrived and Christ has arisen.
Spring has sprung and so have we.

**Jake Jeffs  (11)**
**Painsley Catholic High School**

# Homework!

*Homework,*
What happened to hanging out,
Having fun, messing about?

*Homework,*
What happened to watching TV,
Lazing around, choosing a DVD?

*Homework,*
What happened to staying up late,
Going on the Internet, chatting to my mate?

*Homework,*
What happened to going out around town,
Going mad, without receiving a frown?

*Homework,*
What happened to always being awake,
Not having to worry about the excuses I have to make?

I will tell you what happened . . .

*Homework!*

**Katie Shield  (13)**
**Painsley Catholic High School**


# Alone

All alone in a dark fearful room
With no one to talk to
No one to call 'friend'
No one to share things with
Nobody there, no family with me
A dark abyss
I was alone
Alone
Lonely
I could smell dust in the corner of the room
I felt as if someone was there with me
But no, still alone.

**Matthew Hurst  (14)**
**Painsley Catholic High School**

# It's Not Fair!

Millions of people are starving in the world,
Go to bed hungry and cold.
Then wake up with nothing to eat,
Work all day and stand on their feet,
But when the simplest thing doesn't go our way,
We are the ones who scream and say,
'It's not fair!'

Thousands of people live on the streets,
Relying on others so they can eat.
Sit all day and feel sad and alone,
No place to go that they can call home.
But just because we can't go out,
We start to moan and shout,
'It's not fair!'

We should be thankful for what we've got,
And think of what's good instead of what's not.
And maybe when we're being ungrateful,
We should think more of other people.
So many have reasons to say it's not fair.
And desperately wish for a life without a care,
It's not fair!

**Sarah Lockett  (14)**
**Painsley Catholic High School**


# Loneliness

I sit alone in my room
Outside the flowers start to bloom
Around me I hear no sound
Below my feet I feel the ground.

**Katy Warrilow  (14)**
**Painsley Catholic High School**

# Wayne Insane

There is a boy who lives down the lane,
I'll tell you his name is Wayne Insane.
Well Wayne is insane because of all the things he does:
He sits on the roof when he rides on the bus,
He has his dinner before his breakfast,
He has tomato ketchup for breakfast.
He is definitely a silly billy,
While at school with his mate, Willy.
He walks on his hands all day long,
When on the way home he sings a song.
He comes home, puts on the TV,
Demands his lunch before his tea.
He sits on the sofa upside down,
Then he shouts, 'Let's go to town.'
While in the car he shouts, 'Reverse.'
Mum looks at him and drives up the kerb.
The policemen come, *what on earth*,
*What is Wayne Insane really worth!*

**Emily Dixon  (11)**
**Painsley Catholic High School**


# Loneliness

Walking down the long endless roads,
All I feel is empty and alone.
My family is gone - deceased.
What do I do now? How will I cope?
I wrap my coat around me,
The air is cool and the wind is strong.
Where do I go? Will I survive?
My body goes in the direction of a well known place,
I open the gates and continue walking to my part of the cemetery,
Walking towards the headstones,
Tears pour down my cheeks,
Thinking why? Why did this have to happen?
Loneliness!

**Kerry McMullen  (14)**
**Painsley Catholic High School**

# The Long Road!

Our paths meet along the way,
Not just today but every day.

Is this fate?

Why does my heart skip a beat?
Along the street where we always meet.

We stare into each other's eyes
And smile a smile of hope.
We halt for a split second,
But just walk on by as we both cannot cope.

We get so far,
Then fate turns our heads,
In respect to each other's hearts that we were both led.

Another day, another time,
Would our hearts ever entwine?

It all happened long ago,
Long in the past,
We were both so close,
But in the end it didn't last.

Do you have any regrets?
I know that I do not.
Life is so strange and hard,
However time doesn't stop.

I constantly thought we would be together
And I will always love you forever.
You walked on by like you never wanted it to be,
Along the long road, the road of you and me.

**Stacey Greener  (14)**
**Painsley Catholic High School**

# Passion

My friends and me wanted to dance,
We were really interested and were put in a trance,
So we went to dance school
And danced and looked really cool.

Left, right, forward spin,
The talent show was what we wanted to win,
We practiced long and hard,
Till our backs were as stiff as card.

It was a roller coaster of emotion,
We gave it our full devotion,
In the end our dance was great,
Then it was just a matter of fate.

It was the night before the talent show,
But I could not get the dance to flow,
I could not wait till that day,
'I can do it!' is what I will say.

We did all our make-up and hair,
Then the show was finally there,
It was as scary as a grizzly bear,
'Please let us win but be fair.'

We put all our hard work in
And it was not going to be chucked in the bin,
The dance went well
And nobody fell.

We rocked our body just like Justin Timberlake told us to,
We had accomplished what we set out to do,
We performed perfectly and all pulled through,
Then in the end we all knew that our dream had definitely come true!

**Jessica Hackett (13)**
**Painsley Catholic High School**

# My Favourite Things

My favourite things on Earth include,
Holidays, family and also food.
The best place ever is my own bed
And happy memories that fill my head.

What would I do without my mum?
No clean clothes and an empty tum.
My dad just wants a bit of peace,
When he's not being my taxi service.

My brothers can sometimes be okay,
When they're getting their own way.
Sometimes they make me scream and weep,
I like them best when they're asleep.

I always have fun with my best friends,
Shopping to find the latest trends.
Sleepover secrets we all enjoy,
Talking about that special boy.

Birthdays, Christmas and Easter too,
Lots of presents for me and you!
Discos, parties, getting all dressed up,
Phones, clothes, music and make-up.

Sunny days are always best,
Water fights, swimming pools and all the rest.
But snowy days are also fun,
Snowball fights to make you run.

Hockey, gym, dancing and netball,
Are the sports I think are wonderful.
So all these favourite things of mine,
Make all of my days sparkle and shine.

**Jade Cartwright (13)**
**Painsley Catholic High School**

# Oranges

Their colour is bright,
Their taste is nice,
They also contain pips
And can be eaten in single bits.

They can be made into a juice,
But it causes yellow teeth,
You can even mix it with water,
But make sure it's clean.

If you drink it pure,
It's always sour,
But if you mix it with water,
It won't have as much power.

They look like tangerines,
But they're a lot smaller,
They're about the size of an apple,
But in some cases they can be taller.

They're healthy to eat,
Healthier than meat,
But only to be eaten as snacks,
Now do you see why everyone likes the orange?

**Alex Watson-Lazowski (13)**
**Painsley Catholic High School**


# The Sea

The sea is a little child,
Crawling along the beach all day,
With her little hands and bony fingers,
She cries whenever she's mad
And clings to the rocks.

**Nicola Ball (13)**
**Painsley Catholic High School**

# Where Lie The Answers?

What is heavy? What is hollow?
What is today? What is tomorrow?

What is morning when it rolls into night?
What is the emptiness I feel inside?

What are my dreams? What are these tears?
What are these memories of my childhood fears?

What is right? What is wrong?
What is frail? What is strong?

What are the answers I am destined to seek?
What is this language that we speak?

What is love? What is hate?
Destiny will seal my fate.

What is forever?

**Jade Goodwin  (14)**
**Painsley Catholic High School**


# The Workhouse

The workhouse is a shabby building,
Where people are taken when they are penniless,
The standard of work they have to do is appalling,
Twelve hours a day without any play.

They sleep on a solid bed that is filthy dirty and dull,
They feel abandoned with nowhere to go,
They hear terrifying noises down below,
They are tired and hungry wishing the noise would go.

Gruel is what they eat, apart from special occasions,
When they are allowed to have 2 ounces more,
But that was not enough, some boys and girls died of starvation,
They were split up from their families who sometimes the masters hit.

If they did escape they would still be on their lonesome.

**Hayley Finney  (12)**
**Painsley Catholic High School**

# Ode To Bill

I once had a tortoise,
The tortoise was called Bill,
It was an extraordinary tortoise,
It could levitate at will.

It would hover up and down the street
And people would start clapping.
People would call from their windows,
'How's he do that? He's not flapping!'

Whilst in quiet contemplation,
He'd float just above the floor.
But when he was excited,
Skyward he would soar.

Then my tortoise fell in love
And could not control his motion.
He spun around, went up and down
And splashed into the ocean.

He climbed up to a thousand feet,
But then started to fall!
Fear made him go faster,
Then he crashed into a wall.

Alas, poor tortoise, I knew him well,
He met a sticky end,
I bequeath this ode to thee,
My levitating friend.

**Philip Milward  (15)**
**Painsley Catholic High School**

# It's Not Fair!

Look at that boy over there,
Sitting alone, it's not fair.
Staring up high without a care in the world,
In a ball, he is curled.

He stays there all day and night,
Hoping that one day he just might,
Have a family as it used to be,
Instead he lies there looking at me.

'Here, have this,' I said handing him a ten pound note,
'Buy yourself a brand new coat.'
And so he did and it kept him warm,
He lay back down in his sleeping bag until dawn.

When he awoke, a man stood before him,
'I'll look after you, just wait a min.'
So the man went to fetch his car
And the boy watched him walk off so far.

After a while the man came round,
'Come on now young one, I know you're bound
To want feeding and a nice warm bath,'
And so they rode off down the path.

It's hard that the boy has a great new family
And happy I hope he will be.
I believe he has a brand new mother
And so I hear a sister and a brother.

**Zoe Slater (13)**
**Painsley Catholic High School**

# Somewhere

I am a lost soul,
Searching for the one who will make me whole again.
I don't know who they are or where I will find them,
But I know that they are out there,
Somewhere.

I have waded through oceans,
I have crawled through fire,
I have ridden the wind,
Journeyed to distant lands,
But still I have not found them.

I have cried out and wept,
I have screamed and cursed,
I have prayed with all my heart,
But still I have not found them.

I want to give up,
To rest my aching limbs,
But I must keep searching,
I must.
I know that they are out there,
Somewhere.

**Lorna Poole  (15)**
**Painsley Catholic High School**


# The Train

The train moves fast
The train moves slow
The train goes wherever you want it to go
The train is rusty
Dirty and dusty
You could go to Leicester
London or Chester
Because the train moves fast
The train moves slow
And the train goes wherever you want it to go.

**James Phillips  (14)**
**Painsley Catholic High School**

# The World

The world is full of different faces,
Different ages, different races.
It doesn't matter if we're big or small,
We're all equal after all.
So why then do we pick on those
Who can't afford designer clothes
Or snigger behind people's backs
Plotting things, so they can't relax?
It doesn't take much to leave alone,
To leave people on their own.
Not to laugh in hateful scorn,
Making people wish that they weren't born.
The world is full of different faces,
We should all try to get along,
Helping people to belong.

**Tabatha Snow  (13)**
**Painsley Catholic High School**


# Christmas Poem

C hristmas time is nearly here,
H ooray, hooray, everyone cheer.
R acing around buying lots of presents,
 I ce and snow setting firmly on the ground.
S anta's coming on his sleigh,
T ime to give us a little pay.
M ince pies on every shelf,
A sking for help is Santa's elf.
S hhhh, the children are now asleep.

T ime is flying quickly by,
 I nnocent children softly sigh,
M orning approaches, the children awake,
E agerly creeping, no sound they make.

**Victoria Deaville  (13)**
**Painsley Catholic High School**

# Friends

Friends are very special,
They are unique and individual.
They stick with you through thick and thin,
Friends are very special.

Friends are very special,
They help you through life's journey.
They are there for you when you feel lonely,
Friends are very special.

Friends are very special,
They cheer you up when things get tough.
You can tell them things and they'll give you great advice,
Friends are very special.

Friends are very special,
You can tell them secrets and they won't tell anyone.
You can laugh and gossip about what's going on,
Friends are very special.

Friends are very special,
There are different types of friends.
However you always have a best one,
Friends are very special.

**Amy Dowling  (13)**
**Painsley Catholic High School**


# The Sea

An ocean of memories never to be open,
A chest full of secrets never to be told,
Many questions left not answered,
Where the heart shall lie alone,
The sight of dark glistening water slowly drifting away.

**Rosemarie Brown  (11)**
**Painsley Catholic High School**

# Science

Microscopic monsters
Tiny little fleas
Science is just full of little buzzing bees

Bangs and booms in the chemistry lab
Acid everywhere
In your clothes and your bag and even in your hair

Fatal forces everywhere
Gravitational pull
But in space there isn't any
Like astronauts with oxygen tanks half full

Bloody bones and body bits
The stomach and the head
See these in hospitals
And even under your bed

So now you see that science
Isn't just a joke
Because without
We couldn't even have smoke.

**Alison Eardley  (13)**
**Painsley Catholic High School**


# Hope!

The streets are all quiet,
there's no one around.
You've been gone for so long,
so no hope have I found.
I sit in the house waiting for the day,
'I love you darling, I've missed having you around.
Now that you're back now hope I have found.'
I'll wait till then and pray each day
and when you return them words I will say.
    Goodbye George I'll write back soon.
I'll remember your face when I look at the moon.

**Zoe Hewitt  (14)**
**Painsley Catholic High School**

# Sleep

Sleep, freedom of the mind,
Evil thoughts and worries will be left behind.
The brain wanders casually,
Without a single clue,
The thought of what you dream,
It will just leave it to you.

Sleep refills the energy,
You take every day,
It fills you up, right to the brim,
In every single way,
So you wake up next morning,
To take it on by storm.

Sleep fills the mind with random thoughts
And lots of sea level dreams.
Maybe we don't appreciate
What it thinks it seems.
Maybe dreams are reality
And our reality its dreams.

**Sam Barcham  (13)**
**Painsley Catholic High School**

# The Midnight Moon

The wind blew the rustling leaves
Amongst the towering chestnut trees
The moonlight captured an owl's watchful eye
As suddenly a mouse goes scampering by

Quickly but silently the owl moves
And swoops below with an action so smooth
Clutched in the owl's powerful claws
Back to its nest without a pause

The hatchlings are begging with outstanding will
Here comes their mummy with a deadly kill.

**Paul Whalley  (13)**
**Painsley Catholic High School**

# My Pet In The Alphabet

The letter L is for Lucy
My black Staffordshire bull
Wandering and lonely, her life was so dull

The letter U is for unhappy
In that way she must have felt
In the way she took the hits
In her life that fate had cruelly dealt

The letter C is for cheerfulness
That now she has discovered
Since we adopted her from the animal refuge
And being with us she has recovered

The letter Y is for the yearning
For the love she must have wanted
After the pain that she had endured
She now has a family for her, so devoted.

**Matthew Sargeant  (11)**
**Painsley Catholic High School**


# Witches' Brew!

Children's eyes with chilli fries,
Also the screams of babies' cries.

Animals' limbs so rich and tender,
That I got last December.

Eye of newt, toe of dog,
Also the foot of a toad or frog.

Get me a wart from a frog
And add in that flicker from our bog.

Now we are finished, add our motion
And here we have our magic potion.

**Natalie McCall  (13)**
**Painsley Catholic High School**

# A Cat

If I could be an animal,
I'd like to be a cat,
Most of the time I'd be asleep,
On the doorstep mat,
Sometimes at night I would go out,
Catch a mouse or two,
If I were a cat there would be loads of things to do,
My fur would be jet-black,
My eyes would be bright green,
So when I'm outside in the dark,
Only my bright eyes can be seen,
I'd always be fussed all day long,
I'd be a right spoilt mog,
The only trouble with being a cat,
Is the next-door neighbour's dog.

**Katie Cooper  (13)**
**Painsley Catholic High School**


# The Moon

The moon scatters all over the Earth,
Browsing the stars every night,
It shines more than the sun itself,
Searching the sky at night
And resting in the day,
For better things to come.

It waits, frustrating as it is,
To pounce as the sun lets its guard down,
To succeed its opportunity to light
The sky at night.

As it gathers its friends to shine,
To play tricks with the human mind,
But as the day comes, the moon starts to shade,
But it'll be waiting to pounce for another clear night.

**Aaron Coleman  (13)**
**Painsley Catholic High School**

# My Rabbit And I

As I look at you,
Everything I see and do,
Seem to go out my mind
And I'll soon forget
What I'm having for tea.

Those big red eyes of yours,
Remind me of what I love,
Everything I see and do
Just reminds me of you,
What are you having for tea?

Those long white ears of yours
Sometimes cover up your eyes,
But each time I move them
I soon remember,
How much I love you.

You're my little rabbit,
I don't know what I'd do
If there was no such thing as you,
I enjoy my day
And soon forget
What I'm going to do
Because there is no other rabbit like you.

**Kirsty Buckley  (13)**
**Painsley Catholic High School**


# Starting Painsley High

Eager, excited, jumpy even joyful,
Yet anxious, uncertain, frightened and fearful,
Those were the things that I felt that day,
The very same day that I started Painsley,
My feelings were mixed as I walked through that door,
Now I think of Painsley as my school for five years more.

**Alexander Bamford  (11)**
**Painsley Catholic High School**

# My Parents

My parents only live just to serve me,
Fetching me things that I need, at my plea.
Though sometimes I can't stand them, nag, nag, nag
And make me go to school, which is a drag.

My parents only live just to serve me,
Fetching me things that I need, at my plea.
My dad acts like ruler, 'Me, King Kong',
He thinks that he owns me, which is so wrong.

My parents only live just to serve me,
Fetching me things that I need at my plea.
My mum is so soft, fussing every day,
I would look like her if she had her way.

Parents are weird, of that I am sure,
Knowing this, I appreciate them more.

**Eloise Whitehall  (11)**
**Painsley Catholic High School**


# Night

Night is the man that buries the sun,
His clothes are of satin and silk,
He speaks no words nor smiles nor has any fun,
The way he hunts for children is like a cat hungry for milk.
As he lurks in the shadows which he calls his lair,
He doesn't mean to be scary, he doesn't understand,
He watches over children while they sleep unaware.
He's the one in the dark that'll hold your hand,
He is kind, sensitive and has a big heart,
It's just he isn't very bright or extremely smart.
He's our dream-maker, our night-watcher and our saint,
Now get to bed children, it's getting late.

**Storm Ellis  (13)**
**Painsley Catholic High School**

# Animals

Trotting of the horses,
Scratching of the paws,
Barking of the dogs,
Squeaking of the mice,
Tweeting of the birds,
The noise of animals lingers in the air,
Is this something we can bear?

Monkeys hang from tree to tree,
Elephants slurp water up their trunks,
Here comes the kangaroo jumping up and down,
Crocodiles snap their jaws at people passing,
The fish swim in the sea,
All of these animals are amazing,
But most of them are grazing.

**Victoria Akerman (13)**
**Painsley Catholic High School**


# Space

Weird, bizarre Martians
Flying through the galaxy
Waiting to invade

UFOs fly by
In the darkness of the night
Looking at the stars

Mysterious blast
In the darkness of the night
People looking up

Unearthly they were
From a weird galaxy too
They did bizarre things.

**Josh McVeigh (12)**
**Painsley Catholic High School**

# The Wanderer

Walking on his own
Nobody ever knew why
Until that he died

He walked east to west
He walked so near yet so far
Following the stars

He once had a friend
They both just wanted freedom
From each of their cells

The friend hadn't a name
Some called him Nathaniel
Silence was his way

They both went to town
To stock up on supplies
Here one friend would die

The town was attacked
Nathaniel was slaughtered
Our friend then escaped

He had had a friend
His searching was not in vain
His dragons were slain

Walking on his own
Nobody ever knew why
Until that he died.

**William Smith  (12)**
**Painsley Catholic High School**

# School Spell

Throw into a magic pot,
Teachers, prefects, all the lot.
Throw your blazers in the brew,
Throw in all your school books too.
Add a dash of old bat wings
And through the night the brew will sing.
Throw into a magic pot,
Teachers, prefects, all the lot.

Stir into the steaming slime,
All the bits of old school grime.
Don't forget to add your test,
As they become such a pest.
Throw into the magic pot,
Teachers, prefects, all the lot.

When you've done that, wait a min,
Throw all nice things in the bin.
Grab a toad's eye to bubble brew,
Get some mice tails, spiders too.
Throw into the magic pot,
Teachers, prefects, all the lot.

Count to three, you're nearly there,
Add a strand of black cat's hair.
Witches, werewolves, here they are,
Driving up in snazzy cars.
Throw into the magic pot,
Teachers, prefects, all the lot.

**Zeedee Sawyer-Hartley  (11)**
**Painsley Catholic High School**

# Dolphins Leaping

D olphins swimming on the ocean bed,
O n the glistening surface water,
L eaping out of the icy-cold water,
P laying in the waters,
H uddling together
I n the moonlit waters,
N ever stopping to think,
S wimming into the moonlight.

L istening to each other's call,
E ating all those fish,
A ll those fish,
P laying
I n the fascinating waters,
N ever-ending waters,
G oing deep down into the ocean depths.

**Elizabeth Harper (12)**
**Painsley Catholic High School**

# About Me

H elen is my name
E lizabeth is my middle name
L oud sometimes, other times I'm quiet
E very day I go out and play
N oise till 9, no peace and quiet when me and my mates are around

O n my own all the time
N obody to talk to

M ates always together
Y es, you can work in twos, can I work with you?

O n my own once again
W orking on my own
N ever mind, I always think she will work with me next time.

**Helen Wood (12)**
**Painsley Catholic High School**

# My Dog

There's something about my dog,
About the way she's just there.
She sits in her bed like she doesn't care.

Her bark is as loud as clapping thunder,
Her tail swishes and slices through the air
Like a very sharp knife through butter.
Her fur is a shining gold heaven,
As soft as silken feathers.

She is let out into the garden,
She runs round as fast as the speed of sound,
She is as free as a bird
And has nothing to worry about or stop her.
Sometimes I wish I was my dog,
No care in the world.
Sometimes I wish I was my dog,
My dog Shelly!

**Tristan Bland  (11)**
**Painsley Catholic High School**


# Laura's Poem

'Laura,' my mum screamed,
As soon as I heard this, I beamed,
For I knew who was coming,
So down the stairs I went, humming,
For just as I thought,
Because that's how I was taught,
I saw my cousins standing there
And they had brought me a new teddy bear,
I always knew their holiday would come to an end
And then I awoke as we went round the bend
And I realised it was only a dream,
When my sister began to scream.

**Laura Kinder  (12)**
**Painsley Catholic High School**

# Remembering

As I shut my eyes
In a dark room,
Thoughts buzz around my head
And I remember,
I remember primary school.

Dark, dull rooms,
The teacher's fierce eyes,
A kind smile from a friend,
Just small things,
That come together
To make a picture.

Then the thought is broken,
But then I remember I'm at high school now,
Bright, colourful rooms,
The teacher's twinkling eyes
And a kind smile from a friend.

**Sarah Thorley (11)**
**Painsley Catholic High School**


# Space

The moon is very cold
As it spins through the black sky
Swiftly through the night

Empty and frosty
The big gigantic planets
Spin through the night

The big rounded sun
Is a gigantic hot ball
Of fiery heat

Pluto is very small
Spinning through the cold atmosphere
Smoothly through the night.

**Gareth Harvey**
**Painsley Catholic High School**

# High School

When I went to high school
I felt lost but eager to get there

My head spinning, I felt lost
We met all our teachers, I felt worse

We went to our form classes
And got given a homework diary

But  have settled in now
Until next year comes

I feel better now
I've met everyone

One thing to watch out for
Is the older ones.

**Zoe Fallows  (11)**
**Painsley Catholic High School**


# The Wolf

The wolf stands up high
On the cold and misty cliff
The lake under the full moon
Glistening and shimmering

The lake calm and silent
It glows reflecting the moon's
Glittering rays of silver light

Suddenly a loud outburst
Of sound as the wolf howls
Off into the distance.

**Kristofer Heathcote  (12)**
**Painsley Catholic High School**

## The Day When I Realised I Was A Lot Smaller Than I Thought

I leave my mum and enter the huge school,
Sit with my terrified form,
Everyone looks up as the evil head of year speaks,
Nobody smiles in the gigantic hall,
Nobody except the demon headmaster,
Laughing at his year sevens.

Slowly the day draws on,
Nobody really knowing where they're going to ,
The giants push the vulnerable year sevens around the school
As if we are invisible.

I meet new teachers, some nice - some not,
Will it be like this tomorrow
When I come back for another dreaded day?

**Tom Rowley  (11)**
**Painsley Catholic High School**


## The Wind, Rain, Sun And Moon

The wind can blow all around
The wind can blow up and down
The wind can be mysterious

The rain can be boring
The rain can throw it down
The rain is very wet

The sun can look round
The sun can warm you up inside
The sun's a hot place

The moon is many shapes
The moon lights up the night sky
The moon is glowing brightly.

**Lexie Hankinson  (12)**
**Painsley Catholic High School**

## Decisions From Shakespeare's 'The Merchant Of Venice'

Oh my Lady Portia is true happiness you seek?
Why, yes it is Nerissa, if I'm the one to speak.
Well how about the Neapolitan prince, he was a very good source,
Ay, but he was boring, he doth nothing but talk of his horse.
Then there's the County Palatine, was he the richest around?
I'd rather be married to Death's head, all he did was frown.
How say you by the French lord, Monsieur le Bon?
Oh no Nerissa he was the worst one.
What about young Falconbridge, the baron of England?
If only he spoke the same language, is that much to demand?
What think you of the Scottish lord, surely he's the one?
But when will he pay back his neighbour? Surely he's a con!
What about the young German, wasn't he a charmer?
That's where you're wrong Nerissa, he's even horrid when sober.
Now hurry along Portia, the caskets depend on you;
Get a man to take a gamble or maybe get a few.
Now do you remember the Venetian, his name doth slip my mind,
Yes, yes, Bassanio, that's who I will find!

**Hannah Richardson (14)**
**Painsley Catholic High School**


## First Day At School

First I was very excited . . .
Then boisterous people looked my way
They were bouncy, loud and noisy

Then the teachers had cross expressions on their faces
As they told everyone off
The kids looked annoyed and very uptight
But I had no worry on my face . . .
Because they acted just like me!

**Alicia Starkey (11)**
**Painsley Catholic High School**

# I Met At Dawn

*(In the style of Walter de la Mare)*

I met at dawn the princess of dreams;
Hers was a still and softened face.
She floated through the stars that gleam,
Dark, yet full of kindly grace.

Her gown was black of midnight,
About her head a cloudy crown,
Pure white and streaked with light,
Against her flowing gown.

Her olive feet some slippers bore,
Her eyes shone grey like stars.
Faint lights luminate her steps before,
Changing shape and flitting afar.

Her house is floating in the clouds,
Not a house of solid walls,
But of misty light with rows
Around of fiery balls.

Rising from the shadowy pool,
Springs of royal blue,
Divine with a freezing cool,
Bowing over and sparkling too.

**Rebecca Russan  (11)**
**Painsley Catholic High School**

# Night In The Workhouse

The air in the workhouse is damp and cold
Filled with cries of children and the sighs of the old
The sounds of weary voices and of shuffling about
And of coughing and of snoring and sometimes of a shout

The boy curls up exhausted in his narrow hard bed
And pulls his rough sacking right over his head
He dreams of the sunshine, of laughter and play
Only to wake up to another sad, weary day.

**Beckie Clarke  (12)**
**Painsley Catholic High School**

# Spell To Destroy School

Throw into the magic pot,
Teachers, prefects, all the lot,
Throw your worse one in the brew,
Throw in all your school books too!
Add a dash of this and that
And maybe even your friend's cat.
Throw into the magic pot,
Teachers, prefects, all the lot!

Stir into the steaming slime,
All the teachers' best kept wine,
Don't forget to add your books
And all the school's lazy cooks.
Throw into the magic pot,
Teachers, prefects, all the lot!

While you stir, recite this spell,
Because your school soon is Hell.
Bye to all your nasty friends,
School is over, this is the end.
Throw into the magic pot,
Teachers, prefects, all the lot.

**Katie Seaton (11)**
**Painsley Catholic High School**


# Workhouse

W orst experience ever, wondering what it's like
O n my own here feeling like I have been abandoned
R ather be on the streets than in this terrible place
K eep on being beaten, not much to eat
H ow long will this last?
O ne day's just like another
U nlikely we will ever be free
S urely someone could help me
E ventually it's the end of my ordeal.

**Olivia Shenton (12)**
**Painsley Catholic High School**

# Spell To Destroy The School

Throw into the magic pot
Teachers, prefects - all the lot!
Throw your school books in this brew
Throw in all your homework too!
Add a dash of dynamite
And say 'bye-bye' to school tonight!
Throw into the magic pot
Teachers, prefects - all the lot!

Stir into the steaming slime
Homework which takes too much time
Don't forget to add the fools!
And make your own set of rules
Throw into the magic pot
Teachers, prefects - all the lot!

While you stir, recite this spell:
Make your school a living hell
Only if you like a dare
But if not, forget to care
Throw into the magic pot
Teachers, prefects - all the lot!

Teachers walking in and out
Even if they start to shout
Don't let them become a pain
We all know they're very vain
Throw into the magic pot
Teachers, prefects - all the lot!

Add a dash of dynamite
And say 'bye-bye, to school tonight!

**Rebecca Ward  (11)**
**Painsley Catholic High School**

# Spell To Destroy School

Throw into the magic pot,
Teachers, prefects - all the lot!
Throw your work book in the brew,
Throw in all your homework too!
Add a dash of ink and glue
And don't forget what to do.
Throw into the magic pot,
Teachers, prefects - all the lot!

Stir into the steaming slime,
Uniforms so out of time.
Don't forget to add old ties
And all the loud playground cries.
Throw into the magic pot,
Teachers, prefects - all the lot!

While you stir recite this spell
To make school living Hell
Stir and stir with all your might
Long long long into the night
Throw into the magic pot
Teachers, prefects - all the lot!

All is gone, nowhere is lit,
Forget school and all in it.
This small spell has done its job,
No more school - let's not sob!
Throw into the magic pot,
Teachers, prefects - all the lot!

**Joseph Watson-Lazowski  (11)**
**Painsley Catholic High School**

# Spell To Destroy School

Throw into the magic pot
Teachers, prefects, all the lot!
Throw your blazer in the brew
Throw in all your homework too
Add a dash of paint and ink
And don't forget the school sink!
Throw into the magic pot
Teachers, prefects, all the lot!

Stir into the steaming slime
Snack attack and all the grime!
Don't forget to add the cables
And all the chairs and tables!
Throw into the magic pot
Teachers, prefects - all the lot!

While you stir, recite this spell
Pupils do this very well!
Whiteboards, posters and books too
Wall displays complete the stew!
Throw into the magic pot
Teachers, prefects, all the lot!

When the brew is all complete
Dip in it, your dirty feet!
Boil the pot until it glows
It will clean your dirty toes!
Throw into the magic pot
Teachers, prefects, all the lot!

**Callum Morris  (11)**
**Painsley Catholic High School**

# Teenagers

'Your mobile's going off again,' the wrinklies shout,
They're such a pain.
'Turn your music down,' they wail,
'Do your homework or you'll fail.'

I've got so much to stress about,
This new CD that's just come out.
They say my clothes are far too baggy,
At least my skin's not old and saggy.

It takes an hour to spike my hair
And zap those spots, it's just not fair,
Why do they always make me frown,
When I'm dressed up to hit the town?

I've never got much cash to spend,
So my mobile phone is my best friend,
I always keep it by my side -
To phone the wrinkles for a ride.

'What's the matter with your face?
You're always moping round the place.
Your mobile's going off again!' the wrinklies shout -
They're such a pain!

**Matthew Hall (11)**
**Painsley Catholic High School**

# Workhouse

W ondering what will happen to me in this disgusting place
O ut in the yard
R epulsive smell of breakfast
K icking and beating us frequently happens
H ideously, slowly time passes us by
O utings seldom occur
U sually eating in total
S ilence
E verlasting hope of escape.

**James Sellers (12)**
**Painsley Catholic High School**

# A Spell To Destroy School

Throw into your magic pot
Teachers, prefects, all the lot
Throw your blazer in the brew
Throw in all your school books too!
Add a dash of pencil case
And pumps for a sports day race
Throw into your magic pot
Teachers, prefects, all the lot

Stir into the steaming slime
All the food then add a lime
Don't forget to add displays
And lie them in the sun's rays
Throw into your magic pot
Teachers, prefects, all the lot

Mix it up and add some stew
Then you add some letters too
Drain the iron kettle dry
Then add a tasty mud pie
Throw into your magic pot
Teachers, prefects, all the lot

When you stir, recite this spell
Then pour your pot down a well
Then in the well add a touch
Of fairy's dust but not too much
Throw into your magic pot
Teachers, prefects, all the lot.

**Emily Jeffery  (11)**
**Painsley Catholic High School**

# Spell To Destroy School

Throw into the magic pot,
Teachers, prefects - all the lot!
Throw your teachers in the brew,
Throw in all your school books too,
Add a dash of screaming girls
And teachers' jewellery made of pearls.
Throw into the magic pot,
Teachers, prefects - all the lot!

Stir into the steaming slime,
Things that are made up of grime,
Don't forget to add a spice
And be kind, add something nice.
Throw into the magic pot,
Teachers, prefects - all the lot!

While you stir, recite this spell;
Throw inside the playtime bell,
Why did people build this school?
They could make a swimming pool.
Throw into the magic pot,
Teachers, prefects - all the lot!

Put some text books in the pot,
Watch them sizzle on the spot,
Pour some boiling water in,
Watch them frying in a min.
Throw into the magic pot,
Teachers, prefects - all the lot!

**Hannah Jenkinson (11)**
**Painsley Catholic High School**

# Spell To Destroy School

Throw into the magic pot,
Teachers, prefects - all the lot!
Throw your blazer in the brew,
Throw in all your work books too!
Add a dash of castor oil
And three snails straight from the boil.
Throw into the magic pot,
Teachers, prefects - all the lot!

Stir into the steaming slime,
All your work that takes up time,
Don't forget to add mustard
And some peppermint custard!
Throw into the magic pot,
Teachers, prefects - all the lot!

While you stir, recite this spell:
Throw in the school fire drill bell,
Add a cup of lemonade
And some smoothie you have made.
Throw into the magic pot,
Teachers, prefects - all the lot!

Mix it well so it won't stick,
Add some blood to make it thick.
Throw in sugar and some spice,
Kids don't drink, take my advice!
Put out for rays of the sun,
That's just right, the spell is done!

**Nikki Lamonby  (11)**
**Painsley Catholic High School**

# My Family

My sister is very kind,
She always lends me stuff,
She has an active mind,
But she goes in a huff!

My nan is very loud,
She's cuddly and kind,
She always sings aloud
And always speaks her mind.

Betty is a teacher,
Who's bought a brand new car,
She has many wonderful features,
But is scared of travelling far.

Ges is soon to wed,
In a land across the sea,
With my dear uncle Fred,
To give her away, she has chosen me!

**Tom Sims  (11)**
**Painsley Catholic High School**


# The Box

The box in my back garden,
Is just plain brown and bare,
It is so wet and soggy,
If I touch it, it might tear,
What could it have inside it?
Maybe it's full of old toys
Or a nest of a blue tit,
That box is still in my back garden,
It is still so brown and bare,
I am never going to touch it,
Because I am afraid that it will tear.

**Philippa Oram  (11)**
**Painsley Catholic High School**

# Spell To Destroy School

Throw into the magic pot
Teachers, prefects - all the lot
Throw your head boy in the brew
Throw in all your homework too!
Add a dash of something sweet
And tests which turn up the heat
Throw into the magic pot
Teachers, prefects - all the lot!

Stir into the steaming slime
Maths books you use all the time!
Don't forget to add RE
And the cruel dinner lady
Throw into the magic pot
Teachers, prefects - all the lot!

While you stir, recite this spell
Hocus pocus, all is well
All your troubles will be free
Do your magic, one, two, three
Throw into the magic pot
Teachers, prefects - all the lot!

Place the potion in a room
Where the children will sit soon
Don't forget to run away
It won't be safe if you stay!
Watch from a distance and see
Walls fall down in *victory!*

**Michelle Richardson  (11)**
**Painsley Catholic High School**

# A Spell To Destroy School

Throw into the magic pot,
teachers, prefects, all the lot.
Throw your homework in the brew,
throw in all your school books too.
Add a dash of one mouse tail
and the sky will begin to hail.
Throw into the magic pot,
teachers, prefects, all the lot.
Stir into the steaming slime,
simmer for ten minutes, watch the time.
Don't forget to add smelly socks
and add the ointment for chicken pox.
Throw into the magic pot,
teachers, prefects, all the lot.
While you stir, recite this spell,
bubble bubble for the mixture of Hell.
Add your planner and blazer too,
now the spell should be ready for you.
Shout out loud and stir thoroughly,
prod and poke and mash hurriedly.
Sprinkle in sugar to make it sweet,
now plop in some cockerel's feet.
Throw the school bell and whistle away
and say the rhyme you have to say.
Tear your text books into shreds,
put in three billy goats' heads.
Add a spark of flaming-hot fire
and now this spell will grant your desire.

**Jessica Roberts (11)**
**Painsley Catholic High School**

# Life At Painsley High

Wake up in the morning to my rowdy alarm,
Then fall out of my bed, nearly break my arm,
Put on some clothes, getting ready for school,
Then gelling my hair, looking really quite cool,
Take my earring out as I walk on the yard,
After stealing some sweets, getting myself barred,
Whistle went for form, I lined up in a flash,
Making very sure, I wouldn't be late for my class,
History first, I just couldn't wait,
As history was so awesomely great,
The great lesson that I was waiting for,
Was English as period four,
When the bell rang for the end of the day,
I was ecstatic in every possible way,
Got off my bus and started back for home,
When I got a thought about the Millennium Dome,
If I turned it to a very big football pitch,
I would have to start with a very big ditch,
That's the end of the poem, thanks for reading,
Going to clean my teeth, leave them bleeding.

**Tom Taylor  (12)**
**Painsley Catholic High School**


# Christmas

Looking out of my window,
On a snowy Christmas night,
The silver stars are shining
And the moon is glowing bright,
Snow is falling lightly,
Leaving a heavenly white glow,
Children looking for Santa,
Searching high and low,
Christmas is now getting near,
You can tell by the air
And by the atmosphere.

**Heather Ruscoe  (13)**
**Painsley Catholic High School**

# Spell To Destroy School

Throw into the magic pot
Teachers, prefects - all the lot!

Throw your pencils in the brew
Throw in all your school books too!
Add a dash of dynamite
And say 'bye-bye school' tonight

Throw into the magic pot
Teachers, prefects - all the lot!

Stir into the steaming slime
Homework which takes too much time
Don't forget to add the rules
And throw in all the class stools

Throw into the magic pot
Teachers, prefects - all the lot!

While you stir, recite this spell:
Make your school a living Hell
Turn the tables upside-down
Now you rule, so wear a crown

Throw into the magic pot
Teachers, prefects - all the lot!

Add your school bag, mix and stir
Add to the bubbling mixture:
Pencils, crayons, don't be scared
Like the students ever cared

Throw into the magic pot
Teachers, prefects - all the lot!

Add a dash of dynamite
And say 'bye-bye school' tonight!

**Claire Capper  (12)**
**Painsley Catholic High School**

# Spell To Destroy School

Throw into the magic pot
Teachers, prefects - all the lot!
Throw your folders in the brew
Throw in all your pencils too!
Add a dash of teacher's meat
And in goes a toilet seat
Throw into the magic pot
Teachers, prefects - all the lot!

Stir into the steaming slime
Lots and lots of gooey grime
Don't forget to add the staff
And all of the things for maths
Throw into the magic pot
Teachers, prefects - all the lot!

While you stir, recite this spell
Math's master I'll give you hell
English, science, art and games
Be prepared, I'll call your names
Throw into the magic pot
Teachers, prefects - all the lot!

Make sure you've got dynamite
To give people a big fright
Get rid of all the rules
And all the other schools
No more tests, we wouldn't learn
We laugh as school burns.

**Emily Bettany (12)**
**Painsley Catholic High School**

# On My First Day At Painsley

On my first day at Painsley
I was very scared
I thought I would get bullied
As lots of people declared

When we went for dinner
They let us go in first
I don't know why they did it
Perhaps the other children might burst

Even at the end of the day
I still felt very small
Maybe it was because
The year elevens are so tall.

**Sally Mountford  (11)**
**Painsley Catholic High School**


# Game On!

Sleeves rolled up, laces bound,
We're ready to go to the battleground.
We feel a bit tense as we climb the stairs,
A dried-out mouth and raised neck hairs.
As we turn the corner, my stomach churns,
But as we get closer my courage returns.
Positions taken, the bell to start goes,
Team talk over, we're on our toes.
The final countdown,
Now the battle is due . . .
And I'll be first in the canteen queue!

**Jack Conlon  (11)**
**Painsley Catholic High School**

# My First Day At Secondary School

On my first day at Painsley,
I felt as small as a mouse,
I got very anxious,
I couldn't wait for the day to end,
I made some new friends,
They thought the day would never end.

When we went for dinner,
We went in first,
By then I was very hungry,
I was about to starve,
At the end of the day I felt relieved,
I had got through the first day.

**Sean Locker  (11)**
**Painsley Catholic High School**


# First Day At High School

My first day at High School,
Head spinning,
Because I thought I would get lost.
I felt as little as a mouse,
Then I made some friends,
Which made me very happy.
Soon I was excited,
New friends and I did not get lost,
But then I met the teachers!
We went to dinner early,
So we would not be squished by the big kids,
It carried on like that, which was my first day at high school.

**Sadie Golden  (11)**
**Painsley Catholic High School**

# On My First Day At Painsley

On my first day at Painsley,
I felt really, really small
And to start off the day,
We went into the hall.

On my first day at Painsley,
*I will get lost*, I thought,
But actually it was easier,
Than I'd bargained for.

On my first day at Painsley,
It was so, so great.
I enjoyed every single lesson
And every single break.

**Matthew Tomlinson  (11)**
**Painsley Catholic High School**


# My First Day At . . .

H appy is no one,
 I  feel so alone,
G et in a line, I'm told,
H appy seem the teachers, but not the children.

S cared and uncertain,
C hildren are crying,
H oping it will be alright,
O ne person is smiling, that's the head teacher,
O nly then does the head of year storm in,
 L ife at High School, what will it be like?

**Charlotte Slaney  (11)**
**Painsley Catholic High School**

# My First Day

People are big, I am small
The first thing we did was go into the hall
I met the head teacher and head of year
I was quite frightened, some people shed a tear

But then I met people and made new friends
And then I thought that the day would never end
We went to dinner early so year eights could not push in
We went out to break and made a big din

We went to last lesson
And the day ended
I walked to my front door
And flumped my bag on the floor.

**Daniel Pegg (11)**
**Painsley Catholic High School**


# The Dreaded First Day

As the first day went by
You felt anxious then very down
You get lost and begin to get scared
You make new friends that make you laugh
And that hides what you feel
You enter the dinner hall then . . .
In charge everyone else, it looked very dangerous!
The extra curricular activities are very good,
Try them out is what you should do!
You meet new teachers who are very kind,
They look mean but are just big softies,
The day comes to an end and you feel nothing but happy.

**Alex Bird (11)**
**Painsley Catholic High School**

# Key Stage 3

I arrived at this school,
Trying to be cool,
But really I was terrified.

I slowly walked
And tried to talk
To people I didn't know.

I went to the hall,
Past people who were tall
And wished that I was at home.

At the end of the day
I tried to say
I'll definitely be okay!

**Abbi-Gayle Lindop (11)**
**Painsley Catholic High School**

# My First Day

I was nervous and scared,
I wanted to go back to bed.
As I walked through the gates,
I saw all my mates
And the nerves were just blown far away.

The bell rang at nine,
I got into my line,
As we were sent in for the new day,
Soon it was break
And down came a ray
Of beautiful golden sunlight.

**Samuel Howourth (11)**
**Painsley Catholic High School**

# Titanic

The Titanic sailed on the sea
Its deck gleaming happily
It was a fine piece of art
The lifeboats on it were placed apart
When suddenly the hour was late
People had finished dining off their plate
People were snoring in their beds
People were partying off their heads
The terror struck and people were stuck
The watertight doors slammed straight shut
People were screaming and lifeboats were filled
The unfortunate fled hoping not to get killed
The ship rose up and people hung on
And then the ship floundered and all was gone.

**Aaron Nash (14)**
**Painsley Catholic High School**


# High School

I feel alone, scared, uncomfortable all in one,
I have never felt like this, the room seems to spin.
We are sent to first lesson, the corridor goes on forever,
First lesson and second lesson,
Survived.

Break! Everyone is huddled in groups, whistle blows.

Dinner! Third lesson, survived, we eat in silence,
We are silently scuttling across the floor,
The whistle again, it doesn't seem as bad.

End of school! Finished! Mum asks, 'How did you like it?'
I think, *can I go again, please!*

**Daniel Bayles (11)**
**Painsley Catholic High School**

# The Titanic Disaster

The monstrous iceberg came into view,
'Hard to stern!' yelled the crew,
We hit the beast at a quarter past two
And had to man the lifeboats double time too.

Alas, women and children first,
I had to wait for my guardian angel,
Panic all around, confusion, no one frowns,
'We're all going to die!' yelled a petrified man,
'Shut up you fool and be a man!'

The bow went under like a knife through butter
And spilled over the deck till it was vertical,
So it went down with 2200 passengers and crew
And who survived? Only a few.

**Jack Finney  (14)**
**Painsley Catholic High School**


# Secondary School!

From oldest to youngest, from biggest to small,
A thousand pupils are amazingly tall.
A thousand thoughts rush through my head:
Why am I here? I wish I was dead!

A thousand teachers, a thousand rooms,
I pray that I find my way around soon.
A thousand giants above my height,
Would push and yell and give me a fright.

Finally it's over! Finally it's done!
But rather unfortunately
There's piles of homework to be done!

**Benjamin Cope  (12)**
**Painsley Catholic High School**

# True Love But Hate!

True love was there,
Yet there was no care,
Taken in this wild, romantic dare.

Their love would turn sour,
Not like a blossomed flower,
In less than an hour.

Their love was sealed,
But not revealed,
To members of the family in the battlefield.

The fight was near
And would only bring a tear,
To the families who didn't fear.

Mercutio was dead
And Romeo's heart bled
And wanted evil Tybalt's head.

He ended tyrant Tybalt's tale,
Without turning pale
And proceeded to set sail.

Romeo and Juliet both did die,
Which made their families cry,
As they never had the chance to say goodbye.

**Daniel Hammond (14)**
**Painsley Catholic High School**

# The Sea

The sea is a street beggar,
Strolling around looking for somewhere to rest,
He grabs anything that is offered to him,
Forever he strolls along the same path
And is always lonely on his journey.

**Christopher Steele (13)**
**Painsley Catholic High School**

# Late For School Again

*Bish, bash, bosh*, my family is in a rush
If I don't get dressed in 20 secs
I'm gonna miss the bus
I'm late for school
My mates think it's cool
But my teacher is all of a flush
My teacher started to chant
And steam came out of his mouth
And says we have things to talk about
He gave me detention and this I dare mention
Was very daunting indeed
It's the end of the day
And I won't miss the bus
Because I'm running there at full speed.

**Luke Adams  (12)**
**Painsley Catholic High School**


# Loving

Loving and caring for someone is true,
But what if they don't love and care for you?
What if they loathe you and think you're bad?
This could make you down and sad.

If you try to show them your affection,
You end up in tears of hatred and rejection,
Well if you fit into this place,
If you're down and sad, if that's the case,

Well, just between you and me,
Be nice and be happy,
Don't flutter round like a pigeon or dove,
Just find someone else to love.

**Thomas Whitehouse  (14)**
**Painsley Catholic High School**

# New School

Nervously walking up to school,
I didn't think the teachers would be so cool,
Children here, adults there,
People and cars everywhere.

Cross the road at the lollipop,
Walk into the hall and suddenly stop,
'Hello teacher, I'm new today,
Where do I sit, I'm in 7J?'

Science is the best,
It can beat all the rest,
PE is next,
Because you don't have to write text.

Music, German, technology and art,
Old and new subjects, I can't wait to start,
I like the new uniform and wearing a tie,
There's so much to do, the days seem to fly.

**Nicholas Roberts (11)**
**Painsley Catholic High School**


# Would I Still Go There?

I can hear the wind whistling against outside my window,
Whispering, calling out to me that there will be great waves tomorrow,
I need to sleep to get my rest,
For when that perfect wave comes,
Then I can do my best,
I wouldn't hang back to ride the white horses,
But I'd go on the black, and surf to Hell and back
Even if to fulfil my dreams, first I had to face my nightmares
And to succeed first I had to fail,
I'd still go there,
Early I will rise and late I will come in,
With no doubt, no reason,
No questioning myself what for.

**Helena Stanier (14)**
**Painsley Catholic High School**

# Walking

Spring is here as I go along,
Hearing the birds singing a song,
All the flowers spring to life,
It is the spring night as I settle down,
Walking, walking, walking.

Summer has come as I walk,
I hear people in their garden talk,
The butterflies and the birds flutter around,
It is the summer night as I settle down,
Walking, walking, walking.

Autumn is around with leaves falling,
The sound of fireworks screaming and calling,
The bonfire roars as loud as it can,
It is the autumn night as I settle down,
Walking, walking, walking.

Winter has fallen, walking in snow,
Snowballs all around, throwing, throwing, throw,
Most people get cold, afraid of frostbite,
It is the winter night as I settle down,
Walking, walking, walking . . .
Gone.

**Chelsie Hill**
**Painsley Catholic High School**


# No Escape

N o one cares, I dread every day,
O n my own, isolated from civilisation.

E very day is the same routine,
S trenuous, exhausting,
C ruel and dismal,
A  scrap of bread to last all through the day,
P lease let me out,
E ach day I think to myself, *will I ever get out of here?*

**Nicola Regan  (12)**
**Painsley Catholic High School**

# My First Day

My first day at school was a day to remember
It was a lovely autumn day, it was the 2$^{nd}$ of September

I stepped off my bus without a fuss
There could be no turning back now
As I would not know how
I had butterflies in my belly
And my legs were like jelly
But I had to go into the hall
Where I waited for a call

We went up to form with Mr Bullock
And sat down in our places
It started to feel alright once I recognised
Some familiar faces

The day ran quite smoothly
As time ticked on
But I was so glad when the bell rang
So I could be off and gone

That was my first day finished
I had a lot to reflect on
One thing for certain,
I looked forward to the next one.

**Joseph Blaize  (12)**
**Painsley Catholic High School**


# School

S ome teachers are nice, some are nasty!
C alling out will get you detention.
H omework is awful but does you some good.
O ften teachers storm like elephants and make a racket like seagulls.
O ld teachers often shout a lot.
L ining up for lunch while people munch is such a pain.

**Rachel Fox  (11)**
**Painsley Catholic High School**

# Another Day

I awake in my bed once more
From a dirty mattress upon the floor
It's dark and wet and oh so cold
Only 7 years, yet I feel so old
I'm off to work to earn my keep
Giving chimneys a real good sweep

Up goes the brush, careful not to rush
Next I follow up the tall dark hollow
It's cramped, it's dirty, my face is black
Oops, now I'm covered in slack

Leftovers from last night's tea
Wrapped up in my hanky
Stale bread for lunch
Crunch, crunch, crunch
Mmm, actually it's quite yummy

Time for home as I walk alone
Down the dimly-lit street
I wish there was a better way
But no, it's just *another day.*

**Holly Barker (12)**
**Painsley Catholic High School**


# Street Boy

S ometimes I think, there's a better life than this,
T errified every day that someone will come and take me away.
R eaching out for my mother's hand, hoping she will understand.
E very day,
E very night,
T errified,

B ut my mother would never know what to do.
O nly our faith would guide us through,
Y et we were poor and had little food, *we survived the streets.*

**Emma Jackson (12)**
**Painsley Catholic High School**

# Is There Anything Else You Have Left Unbroken?

You know you have cut my heart
You know you have pierced the mists of my mind
Is there anything else you have left unbroken?

Leave me alone
A childhood nightmare, but this time I'll never wake up
You know you don't belong with me, not here, not now
You haunt me ever still, plodding on behind me
You've devoured all my other dreams;
So just let this one keep on burning
It's all I've got left, I've got to get out, but if I don't
You'll never take my spirit away

You know you have cut my heart
You know you have pierced the mists of my mind
Is there anything else you have left unbroken?

**Hannah Smith  (12)**
**Painsley Catholic High School**


# Workhouse

W hat fate will await me here in this heartbreaking place?
O n the day when I entered, the smile vanished from my face
R estless nights on my backbreaking bed, falling down
                                        an endless pit.
K nuckles bruised where ropes have hit
H orrid screams echoing down the corridor
O nce the torture starts, your eyes stream more and more!
U nder the blankets my thoughts wander freely,
S till I love my family dearly.
E very day is a desperate struggle to survive!

**Danielle Holden  (12)**
**Painsley Catholic High School**

# My Cat Was Like . . .

M y cat was like a race car
Y ou may ask why, because she was

C areful when needed to be
A lways needing more fuel, more food
T elling you when more was needed

W anting, wishing for more speed
A nd not very good with breaks,
S top signs.

L ike walls or people or furniture,
I always knew she was going to collide,
K nowing she would but not where or when,
E verything goes quiet after a while then crash, bang, wallop!

**Charlotte Heron (11)**
**Painsley Catholic High School**

# Back To The Workhouse

In the workhouse it was cold and damp,
It was also full of moth-eaten tramps,
These tramps are here against their will,
Forced to work, they are never still.

At lunch they cannot scoff,
Or they were forced to eat from the trough,
When they fell ill they were certain to die,
They were just told to go and sit or lie,
For in the workhouse you could not escape,
You won't make a confession, the bobbies will take you
*Back to the workhouse!*

**Aaron O'Rourke (12)**
**Painsley Catholic High School**

# Wondering

Wandering across the road
Wondering where I am
Wondering why this has happened
Is it something I've done or something I am?

Wondering why I'm here
Sitting on this dusty curb
Terrified of the loneliness
Terrified of the world

No one to turn to
No one to cry on
The only thing I've got is
The curb that I sit on

Wondering about my ma
Wondering about my dad
Wondering if I'll make it to night
And what sort of life I had

Shy and timid of the other kids
Who I see going somewhere
Behind big black gates
Wondering what lies behind there

Wondering how I will make it through
Lifeless and limp
The day is due
Wondering, wondering, my thoughts despair

Wondering why me? Why here?
Why do I get this pain every time
Food is near?
Wondering, wondering

Wondering, wondering, wondering
The only thing to wonder about is me.

**Edward Frith  (12)**
**Painsley Catholic High School**

# Dark Shadows

Heart pounding,
Fear rising,
Black Satanic eyes stare down,
Nowhere to go,
No one to turn to,
No! Alone . . .

Alone with my thoughts,
Escape - a dream,
Or so it seems.

Skeletal fingers clutch my throat,
In an evil embrace,
Ghostly whispers brushing by,
Like the murmur of a lullaby,
Rasping voices invade my mind.

Oh how I wish I wasn't here,
Here,
Where screams are silent and spirits dwell.

**Lizzie Brough  (13)**
**Painsley Catholic High School**


# Victorian Poor People

S truggling to stand on my frozen feet while
T hinking about what I have become
R ealising that my life is ruined
E verything I have thought and done
E verything I have tried and failed
T rying to push all my thoughts away

B ut always coming back, is the wail
O f my mother as she was dragged away to the workhouse
Y ou couldn't help but cry
S o I ran and hid in a dark place in my mind.

**Julian Maya  (12)**
**Painsley Catholic High School**

# Ellie-May Sleepwalking

Awake, yet not awake,
Asleep, yet not asleep,
Where am I going,
In this never-ending dream?

Past a door,
Down a corridor,
Past a bathroom,
Oh no, not back there!

But my feet keep moving,
As if with a life of their own
And if they don't stop,
Then I just know that I will die.

But how can I die
If I am awake yet not awake,
Asleep yet not asleep
And all I fear is fear?

**Hannah Smith  (13)**
**Painsley Catholic High School**


# The Victorian Workhouse

The workhouse is a lonely place,
Completely deprived of a happy face,
The work is hard, the days are long,
Even the birds have no time for a song,
The walls are bleak, they even groan,
But the people have no time to moan,
There is not enough food for all,
Even the rats think it's too small,
To suffer this life deserves sainthood,
I'd get out if only I could.

**David Goodwin  (12)**
**Painsley Catholic High School**

# Workhouse Blues

Another cold and sleepless night,
My bed is damp, I have no light.
No one here, I'm all alone,
Wishing someone would take me home.

Wandering through the corridors,
Feet covered in blisters and sores.
No one here, I'm all alone,
Wishing someone would take me home.

The work is harsh, very severe,
Sometimes I wish to shed a tear.
No one here, I'm all alone,
Wishing someone would take me home.

My food is lousy, not enough,
Just eating it can be so tough.
No one here, I'm all alone,
Wishing someone would take me home.

Exhausted I retire to bed,
Knowing another day lies ahead.
No one here, I'm all alone,
Knowing no one will take me home.

**Hannah Walton (12)**
**Painsley Catholic High School**

# Dictionaries!

D on't understand all the words in your book?
I sn't it always a pain?
C an't get to grips with the plot of the tale?
T hey're using the big words again!
I s spelling a bit of a problem for you?
O ne book has the answers you seek.
N ot any old book though, you must understand,
A particular one's worth a peek.
R emember next time English homework descends,
Y our dictionary's your new best friend!

**Lyndsey Alcock (12)**
**Painsley Catholic High School**

# The Victorians

The reign and pain of the Victorians,
Even scared historians,
You would normally have to work all day
And only get a bit of pay.

The children had to go and earn a living,
They could go to the pits, then start digging,
Or up a chimney with their brooms,
Better not get soot in the master's rooms.

Some went to the mills
And caught loads of ills,
Or off to the pot banks,
Never getting any thanks.

Once the day was done,
There was no time for fun,
Straight home they would go,
Even though they were tired and slow.

They had their tea which would probably be gruel,
It was cold and runny, how cruel!
Then it was off to bed,
To think about the days ahead.

**Matthew Thompson (12)**
**Painsley Catholic High School**

# The Sea

The sea is a galloping horse,
Racing round all day,
Leaving behind its prints,
Climbing on the rocks,
Then retreating gently.

**Michael Worthington (13)**
**Painsley Catholic High School**

# Expect The Unbelievable

Creeping up the stairs,
Slowly, quietly, no noise,
Am I nearly there?

3 steps left, until,
No, no, he's looking at me,
Scared, me, no way, *ahhh.*

I pelt it downstairs,
Should I go for the back door?
No, the front door is near.

I turn the doorknob,
What should I do? He's near me,
It won't come open, *no.*

I'm getting nervous,
He's drawing closer, nearer,
I turn around, *no.*

**Amy Leadbeater (13)**
**Painsley Catholic High School**


# The Book

The beginning,
New scenes, new lives, new hope.
Development, progression - each chapter
Bringing exuberance, vitality.
The realisation that no tale is immortal,
The turn of every page,
Methodical, routine,
Each letter falling, forgotten,
Like the sands of time.
Each page, each word, each syllable,
Bringing you closer,
To that ultimate inevitability,
The end.

**Jonathan Dranko (15)**
**Painsley Catholic High School**

# The Washing Machine

It sits in the corner,
Big, square and white,
Look on the front, a little green light,
Switches and knobs, they show what to do,
Is this enough to guide you through?

It sits in the corner,
Big, square and white,
A drawer like a mouth for powder so bright,
It fills up with water, it knows what to do,
The dial on the corner gives us a clue.

It sits in the corner,
Big, square and white,
It works in the morning and during the night,
Keeping our clothes from the dirt and the grime,
Saving our labours, saving our time.

It sits in the corner,
Big, square and white,
It deals with our clothes when they are not right,
It rumbles and tumbles, rinses and spins,
Sometimes it even dries all our things.

It sits in the corner,
Big, square and white,
Tumbling our clothes until they're all clean,
Have you guessed what it is yet?
It's the washing machine.

**Chloe Worrall  (12)**
**Painsley Catholic High School**

# Bonfire Night

Bang, crack, crackle,
High, high, high,
Fireworks swirling in the sky.

Squelchy mud trying to suck off your boots,
Frequent whizzes and constant toots.

Bang, crack, crackle,
High, high, high,
Fireworks swirling in the sky.

Colourful catherine wheels twirling round and round,
Ear-piercing screechers making an awful sound.

Bang, crack, crackle,
High, high, high,
Fireworks swirling in the sky.

The smell of gunpowder writhing through the air,
Icy winds combing my hair.

Bang, crack, crackle,
High, high, high,
Fireworks swirling in the sky.

The big, big bonfire replacing the chill of the night,
Many huge rockets fly high out of sight.

Bang, crack, crackle,
High, high, high,
Fireworks swirling in the sky.

**Hanna Mycock  (11)**
**Painsley Catholic High School**

# First Day At Painsley

On my first day at Painsley
I felt really small
And everyone around me
Seemed so greatly tall

I felt I didn't fit in
But I was really keen
Although some people said it
The teachers were not mean

I made a lot of new friends
Everyone was kind
I really enjoy Painsley
I've made up my mind.

**Poppy Holland  (11)**
**Painsley Catholic High School**


# My First Day At Secondary School

The huge school leans over me,
Making me feel so small.
I didn't know many of the children
And I knew no teachers at all.

I felt eager and excited,
But also lost and fearful.
I started making new friends,
But got homework which was dull.

As the day came to an end
And all my work was done.
I knew I'd like it at Painsley
And find it really fun!

**Mark Beville  (10)**
**Painsley Catholic High School**

# The Eerie Wood

The trees shivered, crooked in the winter chill,
The wind played ghostly tunes upon the gnarled branches,
Gnawing them thin,
The steel-grey sky opened and rain began to spill,
All light lost, faded forever into the everlasting dim.

Forever she had wandered throughout the untrodden paths,
Lost, lonely, her soul clinging to torment,
Her mind calls for the echoing memories of unheard laughs,
Bound to her fate to which she was sent.

The wood is abandoned, neglected, dying in times ever-going flow,
But at the heart she shall still dwell,
No one to hear her weeping of loneliness so slow,
There she shall stay, until her tears drown in a sea of sorrow,
Until time itself fell.

**Andrew Robinson  (14)**
**Painsley Catholic High School**


# My First Day

My first day at Painsley
Was good but I was really nervous
At times excited and joyful
But others worried and frightful
Lunch was very tasty and I wasn't hasty
When it came to tasting
When we met Miss Watkins it was really fun
But she was scary and made us want to run
I made lots of new friends
And was reunited with old friends
So altogether my first day was greater than *great!*

**Amy Plant  (11)**
**Painsley Catholic High School**

# Fear

Fear is a funny little thing,
It can make you forget how to laugh and sing,
It can make you yell, shout and scream
And then you wake up and it's just a dream.

Some fear the dark and lonely night,
Where your saviour is the blessed light,
It keeps your mind at rest, the things at bay,
But it's best to wait, to wait for day.

Others fear the boom of thunder,
It makes them panic, makes them blunder,
Or the flash of lightning, filling the sky,
It makes more than babies cry.

Some fear what they cannot touch or see,
When everything must be nice and lovely,
They cannot stand the changes of life,
The pain of fear, the pain of strife.

**Charlotte Salt (13)**
**Painsley Catholic High School**


# Secondary School

I stood all alone as my mother walked off,
No friends, no family, just me on my own.
I entered the building and walked to where
I'd been shown . . .

Soon, my friend was with me, no need to feel bad,
Charlotte and I, it made me feel glad.
No need to feel worried, if we stick together,
Just be kind and sharing and you'll be best friends forever!

The rest of the day just seemed to fly past,
My friendship with Charlotte was going to last!
Why was I worried at the start of the day?
Painsley is where I'm going to stay!

**Katie Boughey (11)**
**Painsley Catholic High School**

*Young Writers - Poetry In Motion Staffordshire*

# School

Why do kids have to go to school?
Some say it's evil and some say it's cool,
Five whole lessons every single day,
With all that stress we should have pay.

It's a good job that we have a break
And go to the café and eat a cake,
If we didn't have break we'd all go mad,
We'd refuse do maths and Mr Linney would be sad.

Break time's great cause we are free,
Everybody's happy as far as we can see
And then the bell rings and we have to slog,
It's time for lines so we hurry up and jog.

At the end of the day we hear *bring bring*,
The bell has rung and all the kids sing,
We meet up with all of our fantastic friends
And it's like Heaven - when the school day ends.

**Alicia Oakes  (12)**
**Painsley Catholic High School**


# The Bonfire Night To Remember!

The blistering flames were flickering, lighting up the pitch-black sky,
Floods of people gathered around the amazing structure
of the Titanic,
The ship flew up into flames like a bomb hitting the ground at
tremendous speed and exploding.
People approached to get a closer look at this huge heap of
cardboard sizzling into ash.
*Boom!* All of a sudden the fireworks flew up into the air filling the night
sky with beaming lights.
What an amazing night that was, we all shared the best moments
of the night with each other.

**Abbey Littler  (11)**
**Painsley Catholic High School**

# Imaginary Fears?

The hairs on my neck stand up on end,
As I take a deep breath and try to pretend,
That the strange noises (someone stop them please),
Are just the trees creaking in the breeze.

Shadows are cast by the silvery moon,
That shines like a candle in the eerie gloom.
The bold, grey tombstones are soldiers in a line,
I hurry on before I run out of time.

Suddenly as the moon goes behind a cloud,
I trip over something on the ground.
Panicked and in the darkness, unable to see,
I hurriedly scramble to my feet.

I look in front of me and get a surprise,
As I can't believe what I see with my eyes.
A whispery, silver 'cloud' stares back at me,
Astonished, I fall back into a tree

And with a pop the ghost was gone,
Did I imagine it? Was I wrong?
For sure, I guess I will never know,
Now from this place I want to go.

**Rachael Green  (13)**
**Painsley Catholic High School**


# Friends Poem

F riends are people who like you a lot
R unning around when it is hot
I  nto my house we all play
E ndless games of Monopoly
N ow it's time to go home
D ashing through the door
S o I slam the . . . *bang* . . . door.

**Molly Stone  (11)**
**Painsley Catholic High School**

# Lunchtime

*Drrrrrr,* that's the lunch bell,
In the queue once again,
I can hear the French fries frying,
I'm excited to eat.

Almost there,
Finally my turn,
Can I have a burger,
I can't wait to eat.

I'm meeting my friends,
There's Tom, he is like a fox
Because he runs like the wind,
Here I am, waiting to eat,
It was worth the wait.

**Daniel Ward (12)**
**Painsley Catholic High School**


# Fear

Fear is like a tiger,
Lurking around every corner.

Fear is like a snake,
Slithering slowly in the shadows.

Fear is like a challenge
You have to overcome.

Fear is like a dark alleyway at night,
Which people want to avoid.

Fear is like a drum,
It hits you with a bang.

**Mark Capper (13)**
**Painsley Catholic High School**

# My First Cricket Match

I was waiting for the toss,
To see the outcome,
Was it to bat?
Was it to bowl?
They got the bat,
We got the bowl,
The match had started.

Ben the captain, opened the bowl,
I was backing up the wicket,
I was to bowl third,
I was nervous as a kitten,
*Thwack*, the ball was cracked over the boundary
For four from fourth batsman,
Then he was bowled from Matt's delivery.

Then I bowled,
First ball was a wide,
The whole team moaned,
The opposition had gained a run.
Then I bowled a Yorker,
He edged it to the wicketkeeper,
She dived to her right,
Wc cheered like mad things,
But she dropped it at the last moment,
Everyone was disappointed.

Then I went to the changing room
To hear the batting order,
I was second with Will,
We got padded up,
Gripped our bats and waited.
It was time to go and bat,
We exchanged nervous glances.

We'd made four runs,
On quick singles,
Will was facing a new bowler,
He had centre stump clean bowled on the first ball of the over.
That meant I was facing the bowling,
For our last over.
Crack the ball flew in the air!
I just survived the catch.

The match had ended,
We got unpadded
And got the score,
We had lost the match.

**Jonathan Wooldridge  (11)**
**Painsley Catholic High School**

# Firework Night

Bang, fizz, crackle and whizz
Firework night you cannot miss
Blazing lights shimmering in the sky
Sometimes it bangs that loud it makes little babies cry
Red, yellow, blue and pink
The flashes so bright they make you blink
The dark sky becomes lit up
By the sparkling lights that go way up

Bang, fizz, crackle and whizz
Firework night you cannot miss
After the fireworks there's all the smoke
Then there's a fizz like a can of Coke
Catherine wheels screeching here and there
Fireworks flying everywhere
Bang, fizz, crackle and whizz
Firework night you cannot miss.

**Michael Jones  (12)**
**Painsley Catholic High School**

# Lunchtime!

I bet you've never been to my school before,
I bet you wish you never will
'Cause my school is the home of, well . .
*Flying food!*

Every day at twenty-past twelve,
There's a riot in the corridor,
A riot in the dinner hall
And time for the
*Flying food!*

Every day at half-past twelve,
There's a queue upon the floors
And queues in the dining hall waiting for
*Flying food!*

I've only ever had a sausage and a hair full of beans,
Jon's always a potato sculpture,
Jenny gets hit with ice cream and other
*Flying foods!*

I only like it on Mondays,
'Cause I'm in first,
But if I don't hurry up,
I'll get hit with
*Flying food!*

**Emily Espley (11)**
**Painsley Catholic High School**


# The Shell Sea

The sea is a shell
Fragile, big and bright
It echoes through the dark caves
With its creatures hiding inside
Away from danger.

**Natasha Sims (14)**
**Painsley Catholic High School**

# My Trip To School

As I waited for the coach,
My knees did knock at its approach.
As it trundled up the lane,
I felt nervous, once again.

As it screeched up for the ride,
I felt like jelly down inside.
I stepped aboard, filled with fright
And wondered, 'Will I be alright?'

Banging, bouncing, with a bump,
Inside my throat I felt a lump,
Filled with fear and full of pain -
At the thought of school again.

Then the school came into sight,
Inside of me I felt more fright,
When it stopped at the park,
I felt alone and in the dark.

But when I saw my friends again,
I felt no fear, I lost the pain.
My mind was still telling me,
If not for school, then I'd be free.

**James Hall  (11)**
**Painsley Catholic High School**


# The Sea

The stormy sea is an untamed lion,
He lashes his tail against the toothed rocks,
Pouncing on the ships lost at sea,
He devours the cliff side with his powerful claws,
Then he calms down, ready to lash out on another gruesome day.

**Jamie Kerly  (13)**
**Painsley Catholic High School**

# The Eye That Sleeps By Day

In the gateway he would watch and wait,
Choosing and changing who'll be his new bait,
Beady eyes, red and raw,
Whatever age he is ready to claw.

Folk stayed clear of the old gatehouse,
They slipped past like a quiet little mouse,
But strangers did not and off they would drift,
Drowned, lost, fell over a cliff.

One Christmas they came, ready for war,
One shell hit the gate and knocked down the door,
Off he fled to another place of rest,
This time the hotel called The Crow Nest.

The owner's child soon was ill and green,
What was the problem? What did this mean?
No one knew it was the fanged old creature,
The owner sold up away from the flesh-eater.

But he still lives there in room 13,
Watching and waiting for someone to eat,
Clutching, clasping, clawing, creeping,
Staring, storing, slowly sleeping.

There he lies in his brown velvet coffin,
Dusty clothing and rusty coughing,
Cotton wool hair and piercing eyes,
Smelly breath and sharp pointed teeth.

No one can stop him from eating this flesh,
Juicy, tasty, a mushy mess,
With a new bunch every week,
Every day he'll have a tasty treat.

So you must stop him as soon as you can,
Or the world will be put into Dracula's hands . . .

**Charlotte Collier  (13)**
**Painsley Catholic High School**

# Things That Go Bump In The Night

Ghastly little ghoulies
Will give you such a fright
Vicious vampire capture you
And eat you through the night

Chains clank
Doors bang
Like bats in the belfry
Sounds bound round

And when the moon is full
I hear the werewolves howl
Whilst in the graveyard
Lucifer scowls

Owls screech
Bats take flight
Is that another ghost I see?
My it *is* a busy night!

**Constance Malcolm  (13)**
**Painsley Catholic High School**


# Love Is When . . .

Love is when your heart misses a beat,
Love is when you feel complete,
Love is when you can see no wrong,
Love is when you want to burst into song,
Love is when all things are great,
Love is when you don't want to hate,
Love is when all the flowers look red,
Love is when lovely thoughts fill your head,
Love is when you're happy all day,
Love is when you don't want it any other way,
Love is when everyone around you is smiling,
Love is when you're on a long and endless journey winding,
Love is when you have a warm feeling inside,
Love is when your feelings you just cannot hide.

**Rosalyn Greatbatch**
**Painsley Catholic High School**

# Alucard

With lifeless wings he takes to the air
The nightmare begins, as he leaves his lair
No crash or bang announce his arrival
For stealth is the key to his survival

His midnight mission is all too clear
He governs the night with invisible fear
A daily feast of blood he seeks
Oblivious as his victim weeps

The marks on his victim's necks are plain
Yet they awake without any pain
Their deathly pallor a telltale sign
Of the hungry vampire's hideous crime

As dawn approaches to his crypt he flees
To hide from the vampire's enemies
His downfall comes from wooden stakes
Thrust through his heart before he wakes

With empty eyes like fathomless pools
He hypnotises victims and silently drools
Soft sensual stare he sucks his prize
Ever hastening his victim's demise

From Whitby he flies in search of food
This demon of the devil's brood
As *Dracula* he leaves his calling card
If seeking his grave look for *Alucard.*

**Jennifer Tomlinson (13)**
**Painsley Catholic High School**

# In No-Man's-Land They Laid

We waited and waited, in the trenches we stood,
Up to our shins in mire and blood,
The enemy received shell after shell,
As we prepared to give them hell.

Our bombardment halted and the whistles sounded,
Up the ladders with fear unbounded,
Bullets tore past us while enemy shells rained down,
I looked forward with determination and a frown.

We charged forward with bayonets fixed,
To take a life, our feelings were mixed,
We kept on running with stride upon stride,
All for our country in which we held pride.

The enemy trench was reached with persistence,
There we found hardly any resistance,
We looked around and no enemy in sight,
Could this be the end of the fight?

Then came in a hazy cloud,
It blanketed the trench similar to a shroud,
It was for our gas masks we all grasped
And those without them fell and gasped.

When it had passed the word was retreat,
It was a failure and ended in defeat,
Attack after attack, little gain was made,
Hundreds dead, in no-man's-land they laid.

**Luke Boston  (15)**
**Painsley Catholic High School**

# On The Day I Was Born . . .

The rivers reflected rainbow coloured flames,
spotlights beamed and bright luminous fireworks set off
with an almighty bang!

Machines turned their old rusty wheels, turning slowly
as nuts and bolts squeaked and squealed.

An old woman with her old wrinkly skin jumped a mile
when she heard that I had been born,
but she jumped too far, she jumped too high
and I'm sorry to say that old woman died.

Clocks went crazy! When it said twelve, it was actually five,
even Big Ben was in a muddle, the clocks were double trouble,
people were late for work, people were late for everything.

An army marched back and forth not allowed to shout and roar,
not allowed to step out of line unless they wanted a big
walloping from the general.

Planets twirled and whizzed around, the aliens must have been
in a clatter, all of that twirling is making me feel dizzy,
I think I'm going to be sick!

On the day I was born!

**Jessica Horleston  (16)**
**Painsley Catholic High School**


# Can You Extend Metaphors?

The sea is a galloping horse
He rears up and down the beach
With his huge stomping legs he trots in the mounds of sand
His mane glistens in the beam of the sun
As he kicks his legs he crashes onto the shore
With his heavy hooves he flicks up the sand.

**James Beattie  (13)**
**Painsley Catholic High School**

# Help Me God

Hindu, Muslim, Christian or Jew
I'm so confused, what about you?
Religious beliefs, people determined to keep,
So many religions, not forgetting Sikh.
Lord, Yahweh, Krishna or Allah,
How come God always seems to be a fella?
If I was God or many other girls,
The moon would be chocolate, the stars would be pearls,
Earth would be peaceful, free from war,
We would all know the meaning of life, what we're searching for.
Everyone is the same, no matter what you believe,
People have a right to speak, a right to live.
So many injustices in the world,
Help me God, is this what you intended?
For the world to be torn? Never mended?
I certainly know and I hope you do too,
Black or white, girls or boys,
This needs to stop, weapons are not toys
And when people realise it is wrong,
The penny will eventually drop,
All this sadness will definitely *stop!*

**Samantha Leighton  (15)**
**Painsley Catholic High School**


# The Sea Is A Raving Maniac

The sea is a raving maniac
It bawls all day
Screaming at the top of its voice
Waving its arms and legs
Occasionally pulling a boat down.

**Daniel Shaw  (13)**
**Painsley Catholic High School**

# The Unknown Presence

The light shone brightly through the cracks in the walls,
The whistling grew louder as it penetrated the halls.
The old, wooden doors creaked and groaned,
As the chime of the bell continued to drone.
I decided to run, decided to hide,
As the heartache I suffered built up inside.
As the demoralised building hollered the sounds,
I longed to walk and leave the grounds,
Towards the forest and into the night,
Along the pathways and into the distance out of sight.
The house was chilling and unfamiliar to me,
But surely this place was my destiny,
Silence was plentiful in which made me aware,
That I was not alone, as I felt a stare.
I sensed a presence within the room,
I was the intruder, I could only assume,
As I was not invited into this place,
It was obvious to me I was an unwelcome face.
Unable to see, numbed with fear,
I desperately needed to get away from here.
So I decided to leave, to go away,
Always remembering my thoughts of that day.

**Cassie Whalley  (15)**
**Painsley Catholic High School**

# The Sea

The sea is a wild boar
It digs up the cliff with its snout
It swallows the rocks in one big swoop
And runs through scores of children
As if they were skittles
Whilst trotting up and down the wet sands.

**Andrew Hewitt  (13)**
**Painsley Catholic High School**

# Tooth Fairy

One late night I saw something weird,
These little creatures, they just appeared!

And now to me it's a regular thing,
When I lose a tooth, one penny they bring!

I lie in bed and pretend to sleep,
That's when the fairies come out to peek.

I keep still; I don't move or shake,
They don't know that I'm actually awake!

They skip around the room and sing to themselves,
They wear green outfits, just like elves.

They nosey in my drawers and read my books,
They giggle, they laugh, they pull funny looks.

Now this is when the fun does begin,
They sneak under my pillow, with a little grin.

They reach for the tooth as gently as they can,
They don't make a noise and they follow their plan.

They don't want to wake me so they tiptoe away
And carrying my tooth in a little tray

I finally get asleep and the fairies disappear,
But when I awake, I cheer and I cheer!

I look under my pillow and guess what I spot?
A gift from the fairies, one penny in a pot!

**Eleanor Ashworth  (14)**
**Painsley Catholic High School**


# Black Cat Of The Night

The sea is a sleek black cat,
Travelling great distances,
Achieving amazing heights,
While being the calmest of creatures,
It can be the wildest of fiends.

**Tom Sandford  (13)**
**Painsley Catholic High School**

# You

Choking in the dreadful pain,
Seeing you turn away again.
All is lost, no hope seeps through,
This fear grows, I'm losing you.

I only wish that you could see,
How much you truly mean to me.
Without you I cannot exist,
I surrender my feelings I can't resist.

I've told you all that I can say,
But still you remain so far away.
My life I see pass me by
And still I wait for your reply.

Will you ever feel the same,
Like you'll never love again?
But all is lost, no hope seeps through,
I know already that I've lost you.

**Marianne King  (14)**
**Painsley Catholic High School**


# The Sea

The sea is a charging bull,
Demolishing everything in sight,
What a bad tempered beast,
Wrecking everything in its path,
Stamping against the beach.

**Matthew Bonsall  (13)**
**Painsley Catholic High School**

# Lycanthrope's Dream

We live alone, secluded,
Outcast from civilisation,
Outsiders from their world,
We lay in hiding . . . in wait . . .

They kill us, we murder them,
Hunters and hunted alike,
We all strive to suppress our 'gifts',
Yet we know it only as a curse.

Man borrows his power from the elements,
We borrow ours from the beasts,
Bound by human weakness,
Enraged by their existence.

'La Luna' brings out our hatred,
Its light the key to our transformation,
Civil man to raging wolf,
Rational thinker to merciless killer.

Our kind do not recall our deeds,
Except by the blood on our hands,
But I am somewhat different,
The man in me witnessed the actions of the wolf outside.

One night was all I saw . . .
The full moon's light enveloped me,
Strength heightened as reason fell,
We set out in packs, the night's hunt begun . . .

First the frosty, muddy ground on my feet,
Then the screams of helpless men,
The blood-thirst quenched, intentions fulfilled,
The return to our homes . . . the feast . . .

Our curse was broken for but a month . . .
Come the next full moon, we will all dream again . . .

**Richard Colclough  (15)**
**Painsley Catholic High School**

# My Charm

The world is bland,
I've been at school all day,
But once I'm home,
The music blasts out
And it's all OK.

The drummer's beat
Is my heart's pacemaker,
He's the rock band's wild one,
The real risk taker.

The bassist's boom
Adds depth to the song,
Its tidal pull,
Enchants the listener,
This cannot be wrong.

Now I'm alive,
Though the song is over,
I've work to do,
This music's my charm,
My four leaf clover.

**Elisa Etemad  (14)**
**Painsley Catholic High School**


# The Angry Shark

The sea is a raging shark,
Rising and striking its prey,
With its shiny wet skin
And with its sharp long teeth,
Dragging the debris in.

**Thomas Mobbs  (13)**
**Painsley Catholic High School**

# The World

The world is filled with injustice,
People fighting for their rights,
People dying every day,
People crying in desperation.

The world is filled with injustice,
Wars, deaths and anger.
People cannot live upon an earth,
Without the need to kill or hurt.

When you see someone crying out,
Don't pass them by or turn away,
Get down on your knees and help them out,
So that they may face another day,
Smiling, laughing, happiness reigns.

**Rachel Hopkins  (15)**
**Painsley Catholic High School**


# Ghosts

Thunder strikes and clouds go black,
All the people in town step back,
The wind, the terrible shadow forms,
In the dusk where it groans.
Silent but heard it disappears,
Where the ghoul cuts with shears.
The night has come it appears,
People around hear a shriek of fear,
Closer, closer, it then swings,
It opens up and spreads its wings,
In the morning, where has it gone?
I don't know, but there's more than one.

**Tyler Starkey  (12)**
**Painsley Catholic High School**

# The Beginning

Everything and nothing is all together,
Just as one solitary, isolated speck.
The fantastic creation is frozen in time,
A time which cannot exist.

How long it was there is unknown,
It cannot be measured or established.
Time is the period between two events,
So when nothing occurs, time cannot exist.

At the beginning of our time it began,
In one instance life itself exploded into existence.
From seemingly nothing, everything initiated,
And both contained and created the universe.

The space time continuum was formed,
Vortexes, worm holes and solar systems created.
But were all torn millions of miles apart,
In a wrenching cataclysmic explosion.

So what are we, within the astronomical cosmos?
A minute collaboration of organisms?
A nanoscopic collection of moderate beings?
We are a minuscule fragment of the speck God created.

So to what background was the speck?
It all exploded dramatically, but what into?
If our universe is unique, why does it function so efficiently?
Everything that has a beginning must have an end, but when?

Will the creator be the one to desolate,
Or has destruction been systematically planned?
Are we the instigators of our own demise,
Or can we change it, will we realise?

**Robert Harding  (15)**
**Painsley Catholic High School**

# I Love You

To the one I love, I need,
Goes out this noble deed.
In the future - after class,
I will marry you where performed is Mass.

In the eyes of God, as everyone will see,
How very much I love thee.
Spend your life entirely with me
And I'll be yours eternally.

Afterlife and into death,
I'll be there for your last breath.
Promise me this, my one true love,
That you believe me, as in the great white dove.

I love you so very much,
Let's look past our feeble looks.
I love you for who you are,
Not for money, nor for cars.

Marry me, when the time does come,
Be with me until we've done,
This entire life of which I do,
Want to spend entirely with you.

**Scott Finnegan  (15)**
**Painsley Catholic High School**

# The Sea

The sea is an angry lion,
Roaring on the beach all day,
His frothing mouth and sharp teeth,
He rips open the strangest objects,
Leaving the carcass behind.

**Emily Graham  (13)**
**Painsley Catholic High School**

# Limericks

There was a young lad called Jake,
Who jumped off a cliff into a lake,
He said what fun,
Got bit on the bum,
So he ran back home for a break.

There was a young boy called Sam,
Who ate some very strange ham.
He got very ill,
So he took a pill
And now he lives in some jam.

There was an old man called Jim,
Who got pricked on the arm by a pin,
He said it really hurt,
So he went berserk
And he knocked over his bottle of gin.

**Michael Tyers  (12)**
**Painsley Catholic High School**

# The Sea

The sea is a stampeding bull
Roaming from shore to shore
Rearing up and crashing down
Kicking cliffs and beaches
Never can be tamed.

**Gareth Davies  (13)**
**Painsley Catholic High School**

# Winter

Outside in the ice-cold snow,
Children making the snowmen grow.
Pile the snow up until it reaches the sky,
While inside the adults all eat hot apple pie.

Dogs and cats all lying by the fire,
Looking up at the Christmas pudding on the table much higher,
Grandma's all sitting in her rocking chairs,
Meanwhile Grandad's coming down the stairs.

The robin on the windowsill,
Looking inside the house so still.
Cocks his little head aside,
And hops away to find the other animals outside.

Beneath the tree so brightly lit,
Animals watch the colours split.
The dusk is nigh,
The moon is high.
And the Christmas day ends with a special
*Goodbye!*

**Laura Egerton  (11)**
**Painsley Catholic High School**


# The Marching Army

The sea is a marching army
Forever fighting the beach
It invades and retreats
With thousands of men attacking the cliffs
And breaking down the sea's defence.

**Joshua McLaren  (13)**
**Painsley Catholic High School**

# A Red, Red Flower

Your heart is like a flower,
Where all of the bells will ring,
Where people get married,
But it only grows in spring.

For I love you very much
And so do your children,
For there ring a bell to me,
Simon, Charlotte and Millen.

So what do you say to this love poem
I write to you,
I love you very much,
Where this flower grows,
I'll pick this flower just for you,
This, this flower from me your . . .
Red, red rose.

**Abbie-May Robinson  (11)**
**Queen Elizabeth's Mercian School**


# The Never-Ender

My sister is the never-ender,
Her voice becomes an ear-bender.

It puzzles me how she can speak all day,
Her vocals scrape people's minds away.

She makes my nan laugh to death,
(I don't know how I am not deaf!)

Some of the things she says make sense,
Sometimes though, she makes me feel dense.

But, I wouldn't swap her for anything,
'Cause whatever I say, she's my sibling!

**Jamie Glynn  (12)**
**Queen Elizabeth's Mercian School**

# Courage

Me and the boat named Courage
Was scared to my last breath
Wondering if it was going to be death.

The triumphant roar of the seas were bad
Me, the courage was dying - sad.
Whirlpools everywhere, all around
Making a clashing, hurtful sound.

But for now a tidalwave came from above
Sweeping the beach like a lover
Destroying me, then damaging Dover.

Then all of a sudden the sun came out
Like a flower ready to spout
So now courage is strong and tough
He can get through the hardest weathers
That are rough and tough.

**Connor Deacon (11)**
**Queen Elizabeth's Mercian School**


# Listen

Listen
Can you hear it?
Hear the voices
The voices of a different world and reality
As our minds shift from this world to the next
We find our mind and ourselves in a place of paradise

Listen
Can you hear it?
Hear a voice
A voice not of time or space

That is a voice of a far-off dream.

**Hayley Murkett (16)**
**Queen Elizabeth's Mercian School**

# The Last Day

Sitting quietly in this room
Everyone is scared to move
The clock starts ticking
One, two, three
The only sound heard is
When people breathe
No one knows just what to do
Read a book and drawing too
Write a letter to my best friend
I wonder would anybody lend
A pen to me to write my thoughts
Of course not, I might get caught
The class is over
The day is out
The teachers cheer
The students shout
It's all over for another year
What's that I see, a final tear?
No one could believe what they saw
'Cause that girl right there who was a bore
She just died right there on the spot
Maybe now they'll notice her
Not.

**Emma Fitzpatrick  (15)**
**Queen Elizabeth's Mercian School**


# Bats

There was a young boy called Matt,
Who owned a vampire bat,
It bit his neck with a peck, peck, peck!
It also bit the cat.

**Stephen Corden  (11)**
**Queen Elizabeth's Mercian School**

# Stick

There once was a stick
Who fell from a tree
A dog picked him up
And started to pee

Once the dog was finished
The dog played fetch
Accidentally the dog's owner
Threw poor Stick into a river

A beaver picked up Stick
And put him onto their dam
Stick struggled to get free
Finally he got up and ran away

Stick climbed up a tree
And made a new home
A woodcutter came and cut his home down
Now Stick is paper.

**Tom Mortimer  (11)**
**Queen Elizabeth's Mercian School**


# The Lonely Days

The lonely days
Full of dull and glum
I always begin to slump
Just before the school day ends
Sir says, 'Stop'
So we put down our pens
My thoughts turn to an empty home
No mum to greet me, just me all alone
The lonely days I try to hide
But they cannot be put aside.

**Sam Jones  (12)**
**Queen Elizabeth's Mercian School**

# The Twin Towers Fall

Disaster strikes across the land
As clouds of smoke utter from the ground
The sky turns black
And flames crackle from the two buildings
That are falling to the Earth
Terrified screams are heard everywhere
Until everything goes silent
*For the Twin Towers are no more*
Homeless people scatter the ground
Weeping, crying and shuffling around
Looking for survivors between the rubble
But no one is left for they are all gone
For many more years yet to come
People will look back on that day
11th September 2001.

**Victoria Thorpe  (11)**
**Queen Elizabeth's Mercian School**


# A Spider's Tale

Once there was a spider called Fred
He ate an insect's head
And with a shout
He ran about
Then in a flash
He made a splash
He went in the wash
And came out very posh
He found a cat bone
And then a hair comb
He then thought of cream
And woke up from his dream.

**Thomas McLaughlin  (11)**
**Queen Elizabeth's Mercian School**

# I Wish . . .

I wish I could fly high in the air,
To travel to cloud 9 or somewhere.

To jump to the moon
And never come back,
Spend all day with aliens and chat.

I wish I could climb to the highest tree
And fly like a buzzy bumblebee.

I wish I could fall ten thousand feet
And land on a giant marshmallow sweet.

I wish I could read a never-ending book
And jump right in for a better look.

But most of all I wish I could
*Just be me!*

**Amie Azarzar  (11)**
**Queen Elizabeth's Mercian School**


# Cars

They can be fast, they can be slow
But that doesn't matter how fast you go

They can be long, they can be short
But that don't matter if you're an astronaut

They're silent, they're deadly and never are friendly
They creep up on you at night, their mission is to give you a fright

Some have sirens, some have horns
Some make noises, some drop thorns

Can you guess what those amazing things are?

**Jack Asbury  (11)**
**Queen Elizabeth's Mercian School**

# The Sad Spider

I live under the stairs
And look at people with great stares
I am hairy
But not that scary

Children scream
With a cone of ice cream
And drop it all over the floor
And their mum shouts at them behind the door

I crawl out
And they shout
'Get away
Away you pain'

They get their feet
And try to squash me
I feel really upset and don't understand
Why people don't like me

I go under the stairs
And cry
My tiny tears

I go upstairs
And hide in the children's bedroom
They get a book
And squish me
And that is the end of me . . .
A small beautiful spider.

**Amy Simmons  (11)**
**Queen Elizabeth's Mercian School**

# Kenning

I am multicoloured
Not a dullard
I am always cheeky
I am peaky
I can speak
I have good peek
I can fly
I sometimes tell lies
I peck your fingers
It feels like you fell in stingers
I might swear
I am like a bear
What am I?
*A parrot.*

**Damien Fitzpatrick  (11)**
**Queen Elizabeth's Mercian School**


# The Blue Poison Dart Frog

The blue poison dart,
Lurks in the rainforests,
In the tropical parts of the world,
With its blue scaly skin
And black, bulging spots,
If you touch it it will sting a lot,
If it stings you, you will die instantly,
It's got a long tongue,
Which sucks its prey into its mouth,
That's why it's the scariest amphibian.

**Ben Watson  (11)**
**Queen Elizabeth's Mercian School**

# The Sun

The sun is round, yellow and hot,
The sun doesn't stay in just one spot.
The sun is the people's read,
All the sun is, is a big red bead.

People have underneath,
The sun is the colour of a dead leaf.
It makes water nice and warm,
It makes flowers grow and also the lawn.

The sun can be very friendly,
But the sun can be our enemy.
The sun can be very bad
And it also makes people sad.

**Nathan Burns  (11)**
**Queen Elizabeth's Mercian School**


# A Spider's Riddle

Creep and crawl
Scuttle and shoot
As they scramble along the silky web
With eight goggle eyes
They're small in size
And have many hairy legs
When they climb on the table
My poor aunty Mable
She screams and dives in bed.

**Matthew Hutchinson  (11)**
**Queen Elizabeth's Mercian School**

# A Tribal Dance

Trees sway in the warm breezy air,
A marbling stream swirls and dazzles as
A blazing wild fire, ferocious, red and hot,
Smoke lingering like a steamy perfume.

Beating out an animal of a rhythm,
Every voice sings a chant of worship,
As sacred as God, they surround their homes with poetry,
Dancing in the long grass in the heat of the night.

**Jessica Lobo  (11)**
**Queen Elizabeth's Mercian School**


# The Pen

Hand lover
Board prodder
Clear writer
The ink never gets darker
And never lighter
Lid hater
Pencil dater
What am I?

**Stephen Ashe  (11)**
**Queen Elizabeth's Mercian School**


# A Car

A car runs on petrol,
It likes to drink oil,
It doesn't like the snow,
Also the rain.

It's got five seats,
Including a boot,
It's got four wheels,
Including a steering wheel.

**Dominic Williscroft  (11)**
**Queen Elizabeth's Mercian School**

# The Theme Park

Fast rides are the best
They make me feel scared
I hold on tight
As we spin round and round
The wind pushes my face
It is frightening
But I still shout, 'Faster'

Apocalypse goes up, up, up
Then drops me down
My belly flops and turns
Until I hit the ground
Some rides make me wet
But I don't care
I still go on again
When I next go to the fair.

**Lee Grieves (17)**
**Quince Tree Special School**

# Central Trains

The driver drives the train,
The trains are fast on the track.
The conductor collects the tickets,
Hear the engine - clickety clack.

Over bridges and level crossings,
Through a tunnel again.
The trains stop at the station,
It is exciting on the train.

**Brett Jennings (15)**
**Quince Tree Special School**

# My Friends

It's good to have friends,
I feel very happy.
They make me smile,
When I feel snappy.

Brett, Brian and Kay,
I like them a lot.
They are my friends,
The best I've got.

It's a feeling inside,
To know they love me,
It makes me feel good,
When I'm with those three.

**Donna Allen  (15)**
**Quince Tree Special School**


# The Fair

The bumper cars go fast
The music is loud
Lights flash on and off
I like it when they crash

The waltzers spin round
Faster and faster
People shout and scream
They make me feel dizzy

The cakewalk goes up and down
Backwards and forwards
My stomach goes all wobbly
Will I ever get off?

**Craig Berrow  (17)**
**Quince Tree Special School**

# My Best Friend

My best friend, Kerry-Ann;
I saw her on Monday,
We stood and talked for hours,
About my love life . . .
Can you believe it?
She's really interested in my love life,
I asked her to pack it in,
But if I ever get married,
I've asked her to be my bridesmaid . . .
And she said, 'Yes.'

**Katie Aucote (17)**
**Quince Tree Special School**


# My Friendly Rabbit

He's soft,
He's friendly,
He has brown eyes.
He's bouncy,
He's happy,
He has white fur.
He is my friendly rabbit.

**Brian Hanslow (15)**
**Quince Tree Special School**


# Lads

Some lads are sexy, tasty and fit,
Some lads are ugly, matted and twits.
Some lads are good to flirt with,
Tease and have fun with,
Some lads I want to go out with,
*But there's plenty I don't.*

**Alex Thomas (17)**
**Quince Tree Special School**

# Skipping

Turn the skipping rope
Jump
My friends hold the ends
Jump
It makes me hot
Jump
All sweaty and smelly
Jump
My heart goes boom
Jump
Pounding in my ears
Jump
Jumping makes me skinny
Jump, jump, jump.

**Samantha McIntyre (15)**
**Quince Tree Special School**


# Bacon

Bacon with red sauce - mmm.
I can smell it cooking, sniff.
Sizzling in the pan, listen.
Now it's done, red and brown.
Stick it on the bread, yum.
Bacon in my tummy,
Tasting very scrummy.

**Kay Ward (16)**
**Quince Tree Special School**

# At The Gym

Doing exercises at the gym,
Strange that is.
The treadmill keeps moving,
So I mustn't stop,
Next the rower,
My feet on the pedals
And pull with my arms,
Then the bike,
Pedal fast and slow,
Finally a stretch,
After all my hard work,
Now I need a drink,
'Where is that bottle of Coke?'

**Joseph Ball (15)**
**Quince Tree Special School**


# Cars

Fast cars, slow cars,
Turning left and right,
Blue cars, black cars,
Driving in the night.

Forwards cars, backwards cars,
Parking at the shops,
Quiet cars, noisy cars,
The music never stops.

Family cars, racing cars,
Driving at a speed,
Bumping cars, braking cars,
I hope I'm in the lead.

**Mark Brotherton (15)**
**Quince Tree Special School**

# You

You always were the one
That made me feel at home
But now you are gone
And I am all alone

You filled me with a feeling
I can't possibly describe
I thought that if you left me
That I would fall and die

Instead I am surviving
Flying like a dove
Climbing higher and higher
Even without your love

I'm reaching every goal
Every challenge, every trial
And would you believe it?
I've even found my smile

Turns out I didn't need you
After all the tears I shed
After all the bad words spoken
Can't remember what I said

But who am I kidding?
This isn't true one bit
'Cause my life wouldn't be a life
Without you in it

You've made me who I am
And for that I can't be sad
In fact for that I love you
Thanks a lot Dad.

**Robert Cregeen (16)**
**St Francis of Assisi Roman Catholic School**

# Homework

The school week comes and it goes
And without fail our homework grows,
A bit of English with a bit of maths,
The RE quiz that made my brain fizz.

My brain needs energy, my pen needs ink
And as you know with homework you need to think.
I write and I write, my hand starts to fight,
There's only one winner at the end of the night.

Page by page the work gets done
And any minute now it's time for fun,
Oh no! I have made a mistake
And I don't really want a retake.

Oh I am done and I feel spent,
I can now play my PlayStation with intent,
My brother beat me to it and he won't come off,
I guess I'll just read my book and slowly drift off.

**Scott Davies (11)**
**St Francis of Assisi Roman Catholic School**


# Show Me My Sunrise

A grizzled bank, eroded by the suns of time.
An essence of glimmer on a desert horizon.
Liquid night perish, filtered by the glow of morning.
You sit with me here, our last dawn together.

They say love knows no bounds. Now,
Those shackles leave me, sometime in the day.
You watch the fading moon with me. Our lips connect . . .
Our final dawn, my love.

The glimmer is in full, you smile at the shine.
Our pain, it melts away, all is gone.
The sun is ours, just you and me.
Show me my final sunrise.

**David Shaw (15)**
**St Francis of Assisi Roman Catholic School**

# The Seaside

My feet in the sand,
It feels so grand.
The sea beneath my feet,
So cool and complete.
The fish and chips,
The sights of ships.
The crowds roaring,
The old people snoring.
The seagulls flying,
People with sand in their pants sighing.
People in boats riding,
Kites gliding.
People swimming,
People in competitions winning.
People in tents,
People from all over the continents.
The seaside is grand,
You can play in the sand.
You can feel the sea beneath your feet,
So calm and complete.

**Claire Plunkett (12)**
**St Francis of Assisi Roman Catholic School**


# Autumn All Around

Leaves are falling all around
Beautiful raindrops are falling down
Hats, gloves and scarves put on
Snow and frost is on its way
When we wake up it's cold each day
I know it must be autumn
I feel a chill go through my skin
I wish to wear something thick not thin.

**Jade Kent-Williams (11)**
**St Francis of Assisi Roman Catholic School**

# Zombies!

All of the gravestones read RIP,
The dead join hands in harmony.
Walking down the streets they go,
If you dare you'll say hello.
They suck your brains if you make them mad,
If you die then they'll be glad,
Because that means more brains for them,
To munch and crunch,
Which is an early lunch.

World population is rapidly decreasing,
The death rate is not at all easing.
Everywhere is deserted,
'Aaahh!' everyone blurted.
Perhaps for now these things have won,
Until another creature comes and does the same as they have done!

**Andrew Mills  (11)**
**St Francis of Assisi Roman Catholic School**


# Face At The Window

What am I on this world for?
Why am I so wealthy and others poor?
Why do I have the chance to make it work
But others can't afford a shirt?
Why am I blessed with my family?
Why do I live so happily
Whilst others are alone?
Others have no home,
Others are so cold,
They have no one to hold,
But there's always something to complain about,
Something to have a scream and shout.
Just look around, how lucky you are,
Others have no guiding star.

**Emma Jordan  (12)**
**St Francis of Assisi Roman Catholic School**

# Football Crazy

The stands were full, the teams ran out
The crowd stood up and gave a shout
The whistle blew, the game was on
The teams were fit, what could go wrong?

The kit was new, the colour blue
We're going to score a goal or two
The ball was kicked, it hit the post
Who is going to score the most?

The striker runs, he shoots, he scored
The flag went up but was ignored
A yellow card, a corner kick
A diving header, the goal was quick

One-nil the score, a half-time hitch
The players trooped off from the pitch
The smell was wafting from the fans
Hot dogs for the waiting fans

The squad ran out once again
They were just down to just ten men
Another goal, we've lost the cup
Oh no! The club's ran out of luck.

**Sophie Hayes (11)**
**St Francis of Assisi Roman Catholic School**


# Autumn

Crispy leaves are on the trees,
You will see the last of the bees,
Ripened conkers fall to the ground,
Children running all around.

Harvest festival time is here,
Winter is getting very near,
People giving food, more and more,
Getting donated to the poor.

**Amy McDonagh (11)**
**St Francis of Assisi Roman Catholic School**

# Autumn

We slowly creep into autumn now,
We see lots of pretty fireworks,
In the wind the trees all bow,
As witches and wizards begin to lurk.

Squirrels are storing lots of nuts,
Summer birds have flown away.
Gardeners are tidying up their huts
And we all have a shorter day.

Though colours are fun,
Yellow, orange and red,
There's hardly anymore sun,
The leaves are all dead.

**Grace Partridge  (11)**
**St Francis of Assisi Roman Catholic School**


# Winter

In the winter, snowflakes twirl
In the icy wind they whirl
Hats and scarves and gloves we keep
Whilst outside the sun gets weak

Lives of plants, Jack Frost takes
He covers them like icing on a cake
Christmas time is getting near
Soon the dads can buy the beer

But not for long the earth is cold
As the rays of light appear
Down they shine and melt the snow
And away Jack Frost must go.

**Monique Handford  (11)**
**St Francis of Assisi Roman Catholic School**

# Horrible Homework!

I really can't stand homework
It is a real pain!
Please tell me what from homework
Can we really gain?

I really can't stand homework
I get too much I'm sure!
I keep on writing and writing
Until my hand's red raw!

I really can't stand homework
It really makes me sick!
I tried to ask my dad for help
But he's really very thick!

I really can't stand homework
It just makes me go ape!
On the other hand
It keeps my brain in shape!

**Scott Storey  (11)**
**St Francis of Assisi Roman Catholic School**


# The Predator

Swirling winds across the globe
Darkness unfolds his heavy robe
The sun retreats from a darkened sky
An owl hoots a sharp and piercing cry
Beneath the cover of night he steals
The predator's stealth he quite conceals
A smooth and silent creep across the ground
Fine movements - yes - but still no sound
And all at once he leaps so sure
The victim caught, he is no more.

**Liam Burns  (11)**
**St Francis of Assisi Roman Catholic School**

# God's Hand

In God's hand sits the trees
That swish and sway in the breeze
The flowers that rock from side to side
Knowing they have nothing to hide

In God's hand sits you and me
Sitting there so happily
Knowing God's love will never end
Securely there me and my friend

In God's hand He holds the world
Every bend and every curl
Looking down on us to see
That we are acting respectfully
Praying and singing to the glorious *He*
That we will be there never-endingly.

**Rosa Berryman  (11)**
**St Francis of Assisi Roman Catholic School**


# My Dad

You'll always know my dad's around,
He's big, he's fun, he's loud.
When we're with him time does not stop,
Swimming, football, that's not the lot.

He played at Villa Park you know,
He scored the winning goal.
He gets us all around his house
And replays his crucial role.

Sometimes I make him really mad,
But I know he's a special dad,
For whatever I say and whatever I do,
He hugs me tight and says, 'I love you!'

**Brendan Murphy  (11)**
**St Francis of Assisi Roman Catholic School**

# God's Love

God's love is shining for me and you,
His power is starting to break through,
He holds us in His firm hands,
Everybody in different lands.

He tells tales
Of Jonah and whales
And of Noah with the flood,
To get rid of evil blood.

Matthew is a lark,
A human is Mark,
Luke is a lion,
An ox is John.

Now you've learnt about God's love,
He'll watch upon you from above,
He will always be around
And keep as sound as a pound.

**Robert Glynn  (11)**
**St Francis of Assisi Roman Catholic School**


# The Vikings Are Quite Nice Guys

When the Vikings came to Britain
All they wanted was to show off their funny hats

But when the Brits saw them
They were scared and ran off
Leaving their money behind

The Vikings thought we'll look after
Their money till they get back

But a while later the British attacked the Vikings
So they ran off and never came back again . . .

**Michael Losinski  (11)**
**St Francis of Assisi Roman Catholic School**

# Colours

Red is the burning fire,
Black is like a rubber tyre,
Green is the colour of the grass,
The colour of the rainbow is here at last.

Purple, orange, red and green,
All these colours you may have seen,
Up above in the sky,
A rainbow shines for you and I.

**Samuel Litherland  (12)**
**St Francis of Assisi Roman Catholic School**

# Use Your Imagination . . .

Imagine a place,
Just like space,
Where ships sail across the Milky Way
And the sun watches TV all day,
The planets race around the universe,
But of course, Earth comes first!
Venus makes some tea and asks Mars if he wants a cup,
But that's enough now, it's time to wake up!
Come back to reality in your own home,
In your own bed, your favourite zone!

**Bethany Blair  (11)**
**St Francis of Assisi Roman Catholic School**

# A Breeze

I walk in the breeze,
With the falling of the leaves.

I walk in the breeze,
With the swaying of the trees.

I walk in the breeze,
With the bumblebees.

**Lucie Williams  (12)**
**St Francis of Assisi Roman Catholic School**

# Dance!

Time for dancing, time for me,
Time for me to feel free.
I glide across that wide dance floor,
I dance so hard my feet are sore.
I love the sound of the music's beat,
I feel the rhythm in my feet.
I love the look of the glitter's shine,
The music's there and it's all mine.
Ballroom and Latin are my favourite,
The memory's there I just have to save it.
I keep on my toes, I spin around,
My feet barely touch the ground.
The lights dim, the music slows,
It's time for the night to come to a close.

**Kelly Whitmore (11)**
**St Francis of Assisi Roman Catholic School**


# Time Goes By

Winter days long and cold,
Funny shaped snowmen large and bold.
Newborn lambs playing in the grass,
Winter days a thing of the past.
April showers to make you jolly,
Not a good time to be out without a brolly.
Summer days full of fun,
Playing on the beach in the sun.
Autumn leaves fall off the trees,
Hedges swaying in the breeze.
November, December, the end of the year,
Everyone's happy, Christmas is near.

**Francesca Weir (11)**
**St Francis of Assisi Roman Catholic School**

# Seasons!

The church bells joyfully ring,
For the weddings in the spring.
The brides all dressed in white,
Is truly a beautiful sight.
The buds sprouting on the trees
And the leaves are dancing in the breeze.
The newborn lambs start to play,
As we approach the month of May.

In the summer the weather is fine,
So we take a ride to the seaside.
Sandcastles, swimming and the sun,
Holidays are such fun
And playing in the pool
Is so much better than school.

Autumn is now here
And winter is very near.
As the conkers fall from the trees,
Soon so will the colourful leaves.
As the squirrels gather nuts,
Pet rabbits take comfort in their huts.
The animals hurry from here to there,
Winter is here, the trees are bare.

Jack Frost calls at night,
It gives the children such a fright.
But all is well when the snow falls,
It's time for snowmen, sledges and snowballs.
As Christmas time comes around
And a white blanket covers the ground.
Christmas trees are decorated head to toe,
We wait for Santa to visit, ho, ho, ho!

**Mia Trueman (11)**
**St Francis of Assisi Roman Catholic School**

# Books Are Great!

Books are great,
So why wait?
You can learn so much
About such and such.
There's lots of fun
For everyone.
Exercise your imagination,
With very little concentration,
To take you to worlds far and wide,
Or bring witches and wizards to your side.
It's a great experience,
So use your intelligence,
Grab one today,
Quick, don't delay!

**Heather Carver  (12)**
**St Francis of Assisi Roman Catholic School**


# James Bond!

007 is his codename,
A British commander, full of fame.
James Bond's a secret agent,
To Q and his gadgets, he is a pest,
But to MI6 he is the best,
James Bond's a secret agent.

Countless missions he has survived,
But even for him, he has too much pride.
James Bond's a secret agent,
If you're a villain, he'll hunt you down,
He will not stop till he's checked his town,
James Bond's a secret agent.

**Andrew Magee  (11)**
**St Francis of Assisi Roman Catholic School**

# Nature Is Beautiful!

In the countryside at night,
Nature glows in gold starlight,
Radiant beauty shines right through,
Endless adventures, but nothing new.

Baby deer and wild rabbits,
Lazing in the sun.
Getting into bad habits,
Having lots of fun.

As playtime draws to an end,
The flowers come out with message to send.
Your life is in the hands of us,
So leave us be and make no fuss.

The message is:
Respect the environment,
Be grateful for your surroundings.

**Michelle Gifford  (11)**
**St Francis of Assisi Roman Catholic School**


# I Like . . .

I like chocolate
And I like sweets,
But I can't stand,
My dad's stinky feet!

I like purple
And red roses,
But I can't stand
Babies' snotty noses!

I love Aston Villa,
Because they are the best,
They're better than Birmingham City
*And all the rest!*

**Elizabeth O'Hanlon  (11)**
**St Francis of Assisi Roman Catholic School**

# The Cat Poem

My cat's called Fame
And I know that it's lame,
But that's what you get,
With my little brother, Bret.
He must have a brain the size of a pea,
To give a cat a name that's as weird as can be,
I don't know if the cat can tell it's a dumb name that she's got,
But if she can, I wonder if she likes it or not?
Perhaps it makes her feel so proud wandering here and there,
Keeping her nose up and her tail high in the air,
Or perhaps it makes her feel so bad and hides in our small house,
While outside, cats are enjoying life and chasing a little mouse.
I don't know, will you tell me whether it's nice or not
And if you can think of a naffer name, please tell me what!

**Sarah Stonehouse (12)**
**The Rawlett High School**


# Cats!

Cats appear to be very lazy,
Purring, sleeping and eating daily!

They seem to sleep in weird places,
Cupboard, shelf and sometimes cases!

Although they're laze as can be,
Asleep from breakfast until tea!

Never underestimate cats,
Because their job is killing rats!

Black, ginger, white or grey,
They are all perfect in every way!

**Rhea Hollyoake (12)**
**The Rawlett High School**

# My Dream

My dream has always been
The same old thing,
I imagine the seen,
I can hear them sing.

One thing I'd like to do,
It's always been the same,
To swim and play peek-a-boo
With dolphins so tame.

I'm a pretty good swimmer,
I'd swim down deep,
The lights would go dimmer,
But I wouldn't want to sleep.

So before I die,
I will swim with dolphins,
When I'm dead I won't cry
Cos I will remember the fiddly things.

Once this is done,
I'll live forever,
Whether it's rain or sun,
Cos in my heart me and dolphins will be together.

**Sharnie Healey  (12)**
**The Rawlett High School**

# Farewell My Love

Dear Rachel, this is your Bert
What I must say will hurt.
My love is strong
But not for long.

I must say bye
For I am to die.
I upset the king
That's a terrible thing!

I said he was dumb
So tomorrow a man will play a drum.
Then one loud bang
And I will hang.

After I die
I will fly,
To Heaven and on
But to you I'll be gone.

You can see me
When I'm free
And you look above
Farewell my love!

**Thomas Peaple  (12)**
**The Rawlett High School**

# Invisible!

I see you standing there along with your friends,
It's as if I'm not there,
As if I am invisible.

I try to make you like me,
It's no use, you don't care,
It's as if I'm not there,
As if I am invisible.

I walk past you to make you notice,
If only you could see,
There are a lot more people like me,
It's as if I'm not there,
As if I am invisible.

You see me standing there along with my friends,
It's as if you're not there,
As if you are invisible.

**Zoe Harrison  (12)**
**The Rawlett High School**


# My Dog

My dog has a waggy tail,
Sometimes I think she's been on ale!

My dog always dribbles and licks,
She's good at football and does big kicks.

When she has a bone she gives people a fright,
But she can run at the speed of light.

My dog is a retriever,
She digs holes like a beaver.

My dog is the ultimate best;
Believe you and me she's no pest.

**Rachel Lawson  (12)**
**The Rawlett High School**

# Beware!

Down the dreaded dim passageways,
Lurking beneath the silence,
The mystery of the incident,
Is being interrogated . . .

But beware the mystery of the dreaded person . . .
He invites many ghouls and ghosts,
To haunt and scare the locals at their expense,
The horror enfolds into darkness of night!

A gloomy silence will stalk your steps,
Whilst merciless winds tangle the trees together,
Furniture is drowned in dust,
The swirling fog envelopes anything in its pathway.

Down extensive corridors spindly spiders spin webs of deceit,
Angry clouds finally burst,
Missing tiles reveal dead bodies,
The cold sharp smell of night enters the room.

What could this be?
Will it lie in wait
Or will we capture this beast?
The horror of the thing will always strike us!

**Amy Hadley (13)**
**The Rawlett High School**


# Opal

Opal is a grey rabbit
And has floppy ears,
She has a big fluffy tail
And her hair is as soft as snow,
She loves eating carrots,
She has a nice big hutch all to herself,
But whenever we clean her out,
She always messes it all back up.

**Charlotte Bradshaw (11)**
**The Rawlett High School**

# The Striker

Thud, thud, coming from my feet,
More and more, the beat of the street,
I turn around and see the dark,
Fear flows within my heart
And sweat drips to the floor.

I turn, I strike, I hit,
He falls to the floor,
Unconscious.

I'm dashing,
Sprinting back,
I stop . . . feel my surroundings,
Time freezes on the spot,
I go from cold to burning hot.

Clatter, bang, wumph, clang
Rattle, crump, splash, tang,
I hear my attacker.

My blood is rushing,
Adrenaline high,
I look above, strike the sky,
A look of shock
And she fell.

I walk away,
Into the sunset,
To find what challenge waits there . . .

**Scott Bennett (12)**
**The Rawlett High School**


# What Is Love?

Love is something that should never end,
Love is something that drives you round the bend,
Love is the butterflies you have in your tummy,
Love is a thing that sends you all funny.

**Jade Woodward (12)**
**The Rawlett High School**

# Night

In the dark of a night, when things change form
And when the sky sends down a thunderstorm,
When the blue pool turns into a deep black lake,
The doors and then the windows start to shake.

The dark green trees, then float up in the breeze
And the wind, like old men, then starts to wheeze,
Around and around the chimney pots,
The wind will then listen lots and lots.

Then all will go silent, the storm will calm,
As the sun rises, the dark cannot harm.
The cockerel crows, shooing the night away,
The darkness has passed, now it's time for day.

The evil tree will turn to friendly oak,
The day is not for evil, for friendly folk.
The night-time has crawled back into its den,
Until it's time to come out again.

**Sophie Reardon  (12)**
**The Rawlett High School**

# Memory Block

Children thinking of their entries,
Talking, talking all around,
So if they have been around for centuries,
Why can't I think of mine?

So many poems, they're everywhere,
Poems that make you smile and laugh,
Poems that make you stop and stare,
So why can't I think of mine?

People finishing off their pieces,
Reading them aloud,
My fist clenches, my paper creases,
I've just thought of mine!

**Rob Nield  (12)**
**The Rawlett High School**

# My Auntie Looloo's Garage

When I go to Auntie Looloo's,
There's one place I wanna go,
In my auntie's garage,
There's so much junk you know:
Washing machines and old tin cans,
Tickets from trains and cars and planes
And . . . purple magic trams,
Plus really old Monopoly games.
Dresses that date back to fifty-six
And books that are even older,
Heaters that well, don't really work,
So the garage is a lot colder.
Banana spray and calendars,
From fifty-nine and later,
Notes from all the ancient men,
That used to want to date her.
My mum and dad just wanna go
And throw it all away,
But I just laugh and say, 'God, no!
Cos it'll all be mine one day.'
My auntie and me go and sit
And discuss my right to junk.
My gran and pops try to buy it back,
But their ship's already sunk
And so has the one on the mantelpiece,
Cos the mantelpiece has fell
And the teddy bear's gone off the shelf,
So it can burn in Hell.

**Chloe Hunt  (12)**
**The Rawlett High School**

# Villa Versus Blues

As you walk into Villa Park you can already hear boos and jeers
And see the anger of the fans as players clash ears,
But I am sure after more meetings,
Blues will have more of the beatings.

Hopefully next time Peter Enckelman won't be playing,
So the Blues fans can have back what they were saying,
Last time the cock-ups were coming free and fast,
Now this time David O'Leary wants to beat Blues and have a blast.

This season Villa have got a player on form,
His name is Angel and he goes down a storm,
Even though he missed a penalty, he's still good,
But some Blues fans say he's stuck in the mud.

Villa fans' support for the club may start to fade,
But with the players they've got, they're sure to win!
But a few of my mates say they should go in the bin,
They shouldn't ever have reason to go that bad.

So when the Derby comes around,
I know the result for Villa will be sound!
The best team in the world will always be,
Aston Villa of course - well they will be for me!

**Jonathan Day  (12)**
**The Rawlett High School**


# A Walk In The Park

I walked along the road today,
The sky was dark – a dirty grey,
The road and pavement, looking brown,
Covered with leaves on the ground,
Refreshing rain fell at first,
Then it became worse,
I felt depressed and very sad,
Why is winter so bad?

**Patrick Lewis  (12)**
**The Rawlett High School**

# I'm Just Me

It started off as any normal day,
Because I walked to school the usual way,
But what I was appalled to see,
Was people being racist to me.

It's not my fault, I can't help my colour,
Just because their skin's a whole lot duller,
But for once I held my head up high,
Why should I let them make me cry?

I don't deserve to suffer this way!
So now's my chance to have my say,
I walk over as proud as can be,
Determined at last to make them see,
That I'm nobody else, I'm just me.

We're all equal,
We're all the same,
Because there's no need at all to cause so much pain.

**Vanessa Ranch  (12)**
**The Rawlett High School**


# My Poem!

I'm sitting in my classroom,
Waiting for an idea,
Waiting for it to smack me in the face,
Even bellow it down my ear.

But no such luck is happening,
Topics are just scrolling through my head,
Music, cats, even friends,
Then I realise these topics are just in my head.

If I get anywhere it needs to be written down,
So now here I am writing it down,
I've finished it now, it took me long enough!

**Verity Machray  (12)**
**The Rawlett High School**

# The Winnie The Pooh Poem!

My big yellow tummy is full of golden honey,
As I stand and talk to little Roo's mummy,
Piglet's small and Tigger's tall,
As he jumps against the 100 acre wall.

Eeyore's building his new house
And Owl's chasing a little baby mouse,
Rabbit's planting some apple pips
And Tigger's even doing flips.

Gopher's digging underground
And Roo's bounding on the mound,
The 100 acre wood are all friends,
Now I bring the Pooh bear poem to an end.

**Melissa Porteus (12)**
**The Rawlett High School**

# Ice Hockey

Sticks smashing everywhere
To make people stand and stare
The music starts and people laugh
As a player gets sent for an early bath

12-0 the score is now
As people stand and shout, 'Wow!'
The mighty Duck's mascot runs on
But the crowd don't know that he's a con

The game's nearly over
They've beat the mighty Dover
The police come in who are armed
And now the crowd are finally calmed.

**Chris Beecham (12)**
**The Rawlett High School**

# The Scary Forest To Another World

Walking through the dark, deep forest,
Carefully watching where I'm going,
I am really tired and trying my best
To not be scared of the fright of dying.

Dark blue eyes shining through the trees,
As my heart is pounding in its rusty, metal cage,
I kept still, but I dropped my keys,
I was frightened because of my age.

All sorts of feelings running through my head,
A few of my questions in my asking is,
All I want is my bed!
What will this thing do?
Will I see my family ever again?

Out came the animal, all fierce and tame,
Black and orange stripes blurred just sneaking towards me,
Then blank!
All I saw was the letter 'T'!
But why? Why the letter 'T'?
Maybe I am invited to tea!
But no, it couldn't be . . . woah!

**Emily Turner  (12)**
**The Rawlett High School**

# The Ill Cow

Farmer Ted once had a cow that was very ill,
So he called upon a professional, he called on Doctor Bill.
Says Doctor Bill to Farmer Ted, 'Tell me what's the matter?'
Says Farmer Ted to Doctor Bill, 'She fell down with a splatter.'

The cow was lying on the floor, feeling really down,
Said Doctor Bill to Farmer Ted as he put on a frown,
'Your cow has got the heeby jeebies,
Try her with these pickled leeches,
Try them with a tin of peaches, she should do a few loud screeches.'

Said Farmer Ted to Doctor Bill, 'See you in a week.'
Said Doctor Bill to Farmer Ted, 'I think I heard her squeak.'
Farmer Ted went to his cow and gave her lots of leeches.
To his surprise, widened his eyes, she let out no loud screeches.
Farmer Ted called Doctor Bill to see what had gone wrong,
He was annoyed 'cause Doctor Bill had gone round to Hong Kong.

He fed his cow more leeches and he fed her more tinned peaches,
He was amazed when his cow said, 'I am not ill, just go to bed.
You need more rest than I do, a doctor I should call for *you*.'
They have solved the cow's odd illness; Farmer Ted just
sleeps with stillness.

**Robert Noakes (12)**
**The Rawlett High School**

# Our Dog, Jake!

Our dog, Jake is very clever
He's the one who'll play forever
He's the one who gets the ball
Our Jake's the best of all

Our dog, Jake sleeps all night
He even doesn't get one fright
Our Jake who is very rough
He even thinks he's quite tough

Jake licks my toes all night long
He really has got a soft tongue
He lies down underneath my feet
And stares at me for a treat.

*That definitely is my dog, Jake!*

**Laura Barton  (12)**
**The Rawlett High School**


# The Alien

Green, fat and spotty,
What else can I say,
It's just my friend the alien,
Coming out to play.

With three eyes on his head
And a long red tail,
He will always make me smile
And he will never, ever fail.

His fat body slithers
And his pink hair stands on end,
I will never, ever hate him
Cos he'll always be my friend.

**Laura Taylor  (13)**
**The Rawlett High School**

# Dolphins

The crashing of the waves,
The whistling of the sea,
Here come the dolphins,
Swimming towards me.

The dolphins are here,
Gliding through the sea,
Jumping through the air,
Jumping towards me.

The dolphins are going,
Going back home,
It won't be long,
Before I am alone.

The dolphins have gone,
Gone back home,
All is quiet,
Now I am alone.

**Gemma Coton (12)**
**The Rawlett High School**